The Counterpunch (and Other Horizontal Poems)
El contragolpe (y otros poemas horizontales)

Juan Carlos Flores

The Counterpunch (and Other Horizontal Poems)
El contragolpe (y otros poemas horizontales)

Translated by Kristin Dykstra

The University of Alabama Press
Tuscaloosa

The University of Alabama Press
Tuscaloosa, Alabama 35487-0380
uapress.ua.edu

Inquiries about reproducing material from this work
should be addressed to The University of Alabama Press.

Manufactured in the United States of America

Book and cover design: Steve Miller
Cover photograph: Image of Juan Carlos Flores's handwritten
poetry taken at the poet's home in Alamar in 2010; courtesy
of Kristin Dykstra, edited by Brian Collier

Original Spanish-language edition of *El contragolpe (y otros poemas
horizontales)* published by Editorial Letras Cubanas, 2009.

The paper on which this book is printed meets the minimum
requirements of American National Standard for Information Sciences-
Permanence of Paper for Printed Library Materials, ANSI Z39.48-1984.

Cataloging-in-Publication data is available from the Library of Congress.
ISBN 978-0-8173-5813-6 (paper) — ISBN 978-0-8173-8837-9 (ebook)

Contents

Acknowledgments

This translation would not have materialized without the interest and support of many people. I would like to thank Juan Carlos Flores and Mayra López for working with me directly on these translations, as our circumstances permitted. Reina María Rodríguez, Omar Pérez, and many other poets in Havana initially drew my attention to Flores over the course of years, enthusiastically recommending his books and praising poetic experiments in Alamar. Francisco Morán urged this manuscript forward when I was just starting out: he requested materials for a short dossier about Flores for *La Habana Elegante*. Anke Birkenmaier and José Manuel Prieto, who guest edited an issue of *Review: Literature and Arts of the Americas* focused on contemporary Cuba, similarly moved this book forward in its early stages by including my translations as well as a critical article; I greatly appreciate the comments I received from anonymous readers as well as editorial staff for *Review* during that process. The Americas Society gave our entire project an unprecedented lift when they invited Flores to read with me in New York at the presentation of *Review*'s Cuba issue: this special occasion marked his first trip abroad as well as his first reading in the United States. We are thankful to Daniel Shapiro and everyone else at the Society who helped with the extensive organizational work necessary for making that visit possible, as well as the effort required to host the event as a whole. Urayoán Noel and Brian Collier inspired Flores to join us for a visit to the Museum of Modern Art, which prompted relevant conversations about art, museums, and poetry. Juliet Lynd, Daniel Borzutzky, and Jacqueline Loss read items from the translations in progress and gave me helpful remarks. Editors at a series of magazines continued to support the project along the way; other translations were published by *The Brooklyn Rail (InTranslation)*, *Aufgabe*, *Words without Borders*, *Sentence: A Journal of Prose Poetry*, *Drunken Boat*, *Cuba Counterpoints*, *Jacket2*, and *Golden Handcuffs Review*. Hank Lazer, Andrew Dewar, Ray Díaz, and the always effervescent Pedry/Roxana made connecting with Flores a little easier on my latest visits. Finally, anonymous readers for the University of Alabama Press gave me questions and comments that were useful for my final revisions, and I am grateful for the commitment made by the press to publishing the book. Any errors in the book are my own responsibility.

Kristin Dykstra

Raising Alamar

The Counterpunch is the second book that Juan Carlos Flores has dedicated to "the poetical resurrection of Alamar," the neighborhood where he has lived for decades. Alamar is said to be the largest housing project not only in Cuba, but in the entire world. The unique history and identity of this very large community flow through the tiny canvases of Flores's poems.

While exploring Alamar in his poetry, Flores has mesmerized readers and audiences by delivering more than documentation. He has created a singular persona as a writer, and his syncopated prose poetry commands attention for its own architecture: a sophisticated blend of written and oral art forms. I'll open my remarks with a short sketch of architectural and cultural environments in Alamar, before turning to a more specific commentary about Flores, his unique cadences, and details specific to this book.

Architectural Alamar was raised as a late twentieth-century "self-help" housing community. Located on the eastern outskirts of Havana, it was one of three building projects designed in the early 1970s to decentralize urban Havana's population and accommodate new arrivals to the region. Alamar offered a site ready for quick implementation of the master plan: eastern Havana already had a network of roads, sewage systems, and electrical services in place because suburban subdivisions had been planned for that area before the Revolution occurred (Scarpaci, Segre, and Coyula 218). Microbrigades incorporating volunteers, who were released from their usual jobs to participate in these communal projects, speedily erected buildings following a general plan designed by the Ministry of Construction.

Today one label sometimes applied to Alamar is "bedroom community," and in this sense Alamar is just one of the many suburbs of greater Havana. But this phrase loses sight of key characteristics. A low-budget construction project, Alamar has provided homes for many displaced and relocated people, including residents getting by on very modest means at best. The neighborhood has been compared to urban housing projects in the United States like the South Bronx; some 300,000 people live in more than two thousand buildings in Alamar (Fernandes 176–177). Most could never dream of buying the goods and services geared toward foreign visitors who come to see the older and more central sections of Havana, although they live close enough to ride into the old city and walk down the same streets.

The construction of apartment complexes at Alamar has attracted a blend of praise and critique for features that continue to shape the quality of life for residents. Specialists Joseph Scarpaci, Roberto Segre, and Mario Coyula outline positive features of the buildings raised on the island by the Microbrigades of the 1970s:

> The quality of suburban Havana's apartment complexes is infinitely superior to the self-help housing found elsewhere in Latin America, and even some other apartment complexes in Cuba. For example, these housing units are larger than those in socialist Eastern European countries. Suburban Havana apartment complexes also include a generous amount of light and air, as well as large green areas surrounding them (even though the landscape and maintenance have deteriorated). (219)

Countering these positive achievements are various concerns affecting residents today. Two that stand out are the profound uniformity of the prefabricated buildings and the under-integration of these residential structures with other types of buildings, the surrounding landscape, and social spaces for residents. Scarpaci, Segre, and Coyula argue that these long-term problems resulted from the particularly dogmatic thinking that characterized administrative structures and planning of the early 1970s: "Varying from the norms or otherwise reinterpreting orders from centralized authority was not permitted," so local talent and alternative ideas were not tapped (219).

The repetitive, impersonal design that resulted for Alamar did not offer a very welcoming environment to occupants displaced from their former communities. For all its successes, then, many people have described the built environment at Alamar as isolating and discouraging. Major historical transitions after 1989 have not helped, as the buildings began to age and reveal weaknesses in construction. While Alamar does represent positive outcomes of a utopian project, then, it also must be seen as a place where lived experience is far more complex than a plan on paper.

The post-Soviet period has added new layers to contemporary life and cultural production in profound ways which must be noted here. Soviet alliances and economic support began to disappear from Cuba in the late 1980s, plunging the country toward a crisis that would be aggravated by the ongoing US trade embargo. The Cuban government sought to prepare citizens for the shortages of what it first called a "Special Period" in 1990.

Continuing through the close of the century, economic realignments affected Havana residents differently in the eastern outskirts than in more central sections of the city:

> If Havana was hard hit by the crisis of the Special Period, then Alamar was even more so. The gasoline shortages meant transport into the city was less frequent and there were longer waits, making it difficult for people to get to work. There were no tourists around to hustle dollars from, and the enclosure of the dwellings made it harder for residents to start up small businesses, like the bodegas cropping up around Central Havana [. . .]. There were frequent blackouts, water problems, and shortages of cooking gas. And for the young people of the projects, there was nothing to do. (Fernandes 176)

Creating and maintaining a spirit of community in Alamar became a key mission for artists and writers in recent decades, a mission that seems to have been all the more powerful for musicians. Inspired in part by musical forms from abroad, Alamar's rap and hiphop artists used their art to galvanize local energies and improve community experience as they entered the new century, while also making a place for critical speech about new marginalizations and exclusions in the greater Havana area. Debates surround post-1989 economic strategies, particularly the surge in tourism and the emergence of a dual economy, which generated divisions so harsh that some experienced them as apartheid. For the high proportion of black Cubans residing in Alamar, disturbing new experiences of racial hierarchy and concomitant police harassment aggravated the economic shifts already uncoupling education from social mobility.

These changes in Cuban life became subjects of significant social critique in music emerging from the community, and creative success drew attention to Alamar in positive new ways (Fernandes 179–181). By 2005 that scene had evolved and then devolved. Many participants in the music scene felt that rap and hip hop had flowered in impressive ways that left a real impact— but were then co-opted by the state, an issue that was current at the time when Flores and I discussed the translation of this book. Significant divisions appeared among musicians, and like so many other Cubans who have sought opportunities through migration, many prominent rappers left Cuba. Outside the island, as they moved into new marketplaces and social contexts, questions of co-optation and cultural impact arose: how could rap and hip-hop function as powerful art forms in the market conditions outside the island? New concerns for musicians since that time focus on how they might seek broader audiences, find new sources for their art, and function meaningfully outside the specific contexts that gave shape to their earlier work in Alamar (Fernandes 183).

The broad contexts discussed above frame the life and writing of Juan Carlos Flores. On October 29, 1962, Flores was born in Mantilla, a neighborhood in southern Havana bordering the countryside. There his parents and their four sons shared a one-room home. Flores's father spent eleven months working with the Microbrigades before he was granted an apartment in Alamar in 1972. Their Alamar apartment was very different than the one-room home in Mantilla. Flores remembers their new living space as having a more organized feel: in Alamar they moved into a two-bedroom oceanfront apartment with a kitchen, a bathroom, a living and dining area, and a terrace from which they could see the town of Cojímar.[1]

When composing his first several poetry collections, Flores had already lived in Alamar for decades. He witnessed historical transitions and debates that make Alamar what it is today and what it might become in the future. On its most concrete level, my statement refers to the ongoing construction of the housing projects over the years; Flores told me that he has childhood memories of seeing the Microbrigades raise ever more of Alamar's numerous buildings around him. On a more abstract plane, historical transitions mean the "accumulation of crises and transitions" that began with the disintegration of the Soviet Union during his adulthood: "an accumulation, that is, of pasts to be interrogated and futures open to question" (Birkenmaier and Whitfield 1). If we turn specifically to cultural expression, there is a third register to explore: Flores participated in the rise of the new cultural scene in Alamar. Like many poets from the Havana area, he took an interest in the achievements and aesthetics of Alamar's musicians.

Working towards a parallel cultural renaissance for writing in eastern Havana, Flores has explored interdisciplinary connections by collaborating with musicians, artists, and other writers from the area. Lizabel Mónica writes about this aspect of his work, which is all the more interesting due to Flores's participation in recording projects. Audio and video renditions of the poems help to demonstrate the multidimensional qualities of his work.[2] Mónica emphasizes the prevalence of the public sphere in *The*

Counterpunch, where the speakers' voices link to a collective space, rarely presenting a lyric voice in isolation.

This boundary between the collective and the individual, the public and the private, can be explored in multiple ways in the book. For my part, because I discussed the poems with Flores with a focus on aspects that are designed for the page, I find that his work is not adequately described by the phrase "spoken word" or with direct reference to the slam circuit, performative variants that have become fairly well established in the US and elsewhere. Flores's poetry, with its dual functionality as performance text and written text, is most striking because of its doubly successful artistry.

On the page, thematic components bring richness to the reading experience. Flores's brief but pointed poems include gestures toward the built environment, notes about the diversity of the local population, and responses to the changing economic conditions affecting community life. "The smith," for example, uses dark humor to register the lack of value of the Cuban peso in a post-Soviet decade in contrast to foreign currencies. His work also contains conscious references to the birth of new forms of cultural expression. In Flores's poetic Alamar, where dumpster divers ply their trade in order to survive, "there are unused wastelands, where pedestrians from the neighborhood throw debris from their daily lives and among weeds, the first mushroom rises for a new civility, not yet included on maps of the counterculture" ("The diver"). As Flores and I discussed during the translation of this poem, this imagery crystallizes into an aesthetic proposition—the poem becomes a prompt for readers to reflect on *The Counterpunch* as a whole as a countercultural gesture.

I've speculated elsewhere that the notoriously uniform built environment at Alamar may have influenced Flores's drive to construct his unusually repetitive poetic spaces, within which we discover the vitality and sorrows of people who inhabit them.[3] However, Flores did not talk about his work in this way. He was more likely to speak with me about topics such as the simplicity of his lifestyle. Through this notion, simplicity, he explained that he lived in humble circumstances, did not hold a job due to long-term medical limitations, and thrived on daily routines like getting up every morning to write poems at home with his dog, Luna, at his side.

This emphasis complements the reality that Flores works from the position of an amateur and outsider writer. His outsider status presents a striking contrast to other accomplished writers publishing their work alongside him, in the same venues: they have long been formally recognized as members of Cuba's National Union of Writers and Artists. With his status in mind, it's worth considering the kind of meaning given to amateurism by Hank Lazer, who has observed that outsider artist amateurism may intersect with philosophy in ways highly productive for poetry. Lazer puts special emphasis on love: "*Amor* is the root word for amateur, a term which I do not use in a derogatory sense" (Spaar). In this sense, writing is a profession and a commitment for Flores whether or not the state grants him a formal title or job description. Indeed, Flores has admitted in our conversations that his "simple" image is not so much a truth as the outline for a persona, an identity for interacting with the world. A semi-fictional self or persona enables the writer to intervene in public space from specific angles, and to create a sort of unreal and specifically estranged space, an irreality, Flores's Alamar of the mind.

However, the outsider image can be deceiving, especially if it causes readers to swing toward that stereotype of the poet long established in English-language culture as a lone figure writing a new self in the silences of a garret. I do not accept Flores's claim to "simplicity" at face value. For all the ways we may recognize a real outsiderdom, indicating the minimal scope of his daily routines inside a single Alamar apartment, Flores's brand of minimalism emerges out of sophisticated intersections and a long-term commitment to writing. His writing taps into worlds well outside the walls of his apartment, and he has actively pursued cultural connections with many individuals and a set of significant groups. In addition to paying attention to local musical networks and art forms, which I imagine will be discussed more by critics attending to his poetry in the near future, Flores eventually talked with me about how he found a sort of home in works by composers John Cage and Philip Glass, in canvases by abstract and minimalist painters, and in the international legacy of the prose poem.

It took decades for Flores to discover and synthesize these influences. When he first began to write at the age of fifteen, he tells me, he kept journal entries and wrote stories. By the time he was eighteen he was serving in the military and started to write poems. At age twenty he got his first taste of a specifically literary community. One of his friends from Alamar, Miguel Sabater, took him to a writing workshop. This workshop was offered at a public library operated out of a historic home where one of Cuba's most famous twentieth-century poets had once lived: José Lezama Lima. Flores remembers that participants met every Wednesday at the library to read and discuss their compositions.

His growing enthusiasm for poetic community led Flores to friendships with Almelio Calderón and Jorge Alberto Aguiar, through whom his literary world continued to expand. They introduced Flores to other writers now well known for their contributions to contemporary Cuban literature: Antonio José Ponte, Rolando Sánchez Mejías, Francisco Morán, and Pedro Marqués de Armas. In 1990 Flores met Reina María Rodríguez, a poet who ran an alternative literary salon out of her rooftop apartment in the city, when Calderón took him to her home. Flores thus figured out how a writer from Alamar could become part of greater Havana's cultural scene, gradually building connections around the city. Founded in 1519, Havana has a long, impressive, cosmopolitan cultural history and diverse contemporary initiatives. Thanks to his early interest in literary workshops, events, and friendships, Flores has now carried out projects with groups in the more central part of the city, so his trajectory of development demonstrates how an excessive emphasis on the poet's isolation would be misleading.

Along the same lines, the Torre de Letras (Tower of Letters) deserves mention here because it was the first Cuban organization to publish his collection *The Counterpunch* in a small, handmade edition. The book was subsequently released with a more conventional print run by the larger publisher Letras Cubanas. Led by Reina María Rodríguez and (until recently) Jorge Miralles, the Torre de Letras group has organized lectures and workshops for writers for many years—some taking place at Rodríguez's famous rooftop home and others in buildings around the city. Their goals are to enable dialogue and growth amongst the city's writers and to share literary resources that individual writers like Flores could not otherwise access. As occasional supplies become available, they create editions featuring new literature and translations—that is, the Torre de Letras publishing project circulates these texts while they're still relatively new, allowing writers access to much-needed developmental dialogue despite severe economic limitations that have restricted and slowed the activities of larger publishers. The Torre was granted space at a couple of different buildings in Old Havana, and it is linked to the Cuban Book

Institute. Formerly meeting on the top floor of the Palacio del Segundo Cabo, where Torre participants benefited from a generous space complete with a real tower overlooking a famous plaza in the old city, it was reassigned in 2010 to a miniscule room located high in the tallest building on Obispo Street. Rodríguez continued to offer activities despite the fact that this loss of space left the majority of would-be participants standing ever farther out in the hallway and stairwell, a problem about which other writers began to complain. The many activities offered by the group over the years have been essential, allowing Flores and his peers to swap ideas with writers from the area and abroad.

Another important resource developed closer to home for Flores and does not rely on conventional print visions for poetry: his collaboration with an Alamar-based arts collective, OMNI-Zona Franca, which he described to me during various meetings. In the late 1990s, noting the energy generated by the alternative writers' groups in the more central areas of Havana, Flores and others decided to create an organization based in Alamar. They began performing poetry as a group, dubbed Zona Franca. This eventually merged with OMNI, a group comprised of painters and sculptors. Flores initially led the group, then passed the role on to others; the membership of OMNI-Zona Franca shifted over time to include many participants. Their performances have taken place in spaces ranging from city buses to the local rap festivals and beyond. The group organized an annual event in Alamar called "Poesía sin fin" (Poetry without End), to which officials have sometimes granted a public venue. Permission has also sometimes been denied, forcing the writers to present in private homes. With these nontraditional and performance-oriented projects in mind, the other layer of the written poetry in *The Counterpunch* springs into relief. Flores's prose poetry acquires its second life as a script for performance, and Alamar offered the best site for exploring that potential in his work.

In Alamar Flores also found collaborative opportunities involving low-budget and erratically emergent technologies. While resources have been very limited in the area and Internet connectivity have been extremely low for Cuba as a whole, Flores worked with various people on audio and video projects. There is a DVD associated with the Spanish-language version of *The Counterpunch*: produced by Miriam Real, it blends his readings of poems from the book with music (some composed, some mixed) by Tony Carreras and Emilio Vega. Copies are limited and, given the embargo, they were difficult to access in the United States as I prepared this edition. However, its opening trailer, audio excerpts, and an extended video with remarks from Flores and the musicians about the making of the DVD appear online.[4] Collaborative projects like this one allow Flores to experiment with multimedia options that surface in the neighborhood, even though he doesn't operate the technologies himself.

In a discussion of *The Counterpunch*, it is also important acknowledge roles played by Mayra López in the book's material production. Flores was careful to credit his former long-term partner López for her support. Without her he would surely have created poetry, but it would have happened differently. For the creation of the Spanish-language text, and then for facilitating our dialogues during my translation process, she was a translator in ways both literal and symbolic. López worked at points of intersection between Flores and the outside world.

The most basic intersection involved the transformation of poems from written to print objects. Flores—who was not in the least comfortable using a keyboard—wrote these poems by hand. (I photographed samples of his handwriting during a visit to their home, and designer Steve Miller used one of those photographs to create the cover of this edition.[5]) López would type up these drafts and, over time, enter Flores's revisions as his book projects developed. Flores told me that he considered this step through López' writing to be a kind of translation and specified that he had a related notion in mind when composing the opening poem of his book, "Manuscritos" ("Manuscripts"). While that poem could be read quite effectively as a commentary on diaspora, Flores finds in it a representation of his own creative process: "All of these poems were handwritten and their first translation begins with the conversion into letters typed on a computer," he stated ("todos estos poemas fueron escritos a mano y que su primera traducción comienza al convertirlos en letra tipográfica en una computadora").

Meanwhile, for personal and medical reasons Flores was not comfortable making many trips to Havana from Alamar. López sometimes ran literary errands, such as helping visiting writers find their way to Flores in Alamar (where cab drivers have a hard time locating specific buildings among the hundreds of identical structures); and she periodically urged him out of his routines, into the city. She also assisted Flores with the use of email, a significant resource that would otherwise be lost to someone who didn't use computers or hold a job permitting him to have an email account in Cuba during those years. López not only made our communications possible but also helped Flores to interact with friends, poets, editors, and organizations in various countries. However, the services the couple could access were very limited. For example, López had an email account through an intranet system run by the government, but that system wasn't integrated with Internet access. Their type of access differed greatly from what writers in the United States and many other countries tended to take for granted, and it was difficult to share our digital publications with them, such as selected translations published by *The Brooklyn Rail* (*InTranslation*) and *La Habana Elegante*. Still, their access made a difference despite the limitations, allowing Flores to participate in poetry worlds that would otherwise be denied to him.

Access to cultural resources, in general, is a topic worthy of an entire future study. As I have briefly noted here, Havana is a richly cosmopolitan city with a significant literary history. Cuba's literacy campaign and state sponsorship of literary publishing after 1959 enabled the development of a highly educated community with international interests. At the same time, the economic difficulties of recent decades have had a major impact. The literary community is partially dispersed into diaspora—in fact, nearly all of the poets I named as important peers for Flores in past decades had left the island before or during the time I was writing my translation, even if they maintained connections to friends and family there (Calderón, Aguiar, Ponte, Sánchez, Morán, Marqués, Miralles and others). Back on the island, many poets continued their writing, but shortages of resources continued to curtail activity, and book imports were erratic—meaning that Flores had rarely or never seen works by poets and musicians whom English-language readers might assume to be central to his pantheon. Gertrude Stein is one such example, or in the contemporary period, Ron Silliman. Flores told me he once read a Stein novel but remembers nothing about it, and while he would have liked to see translations of her poetry, he had never succeeded in obtaining them. Meanwhile, Flores had never heard of Silliman, though some other poets in the area are loosely familiar with his work. Flores does not read languages other than Spanish, and he added that in his own experience literary translations didn't seem to be published very frequently in Cuba, so if he wanted to read literature in translation he had to hope that someone would bring him (often costly) editions published in other countries.

Music also arrived in erratic patterns. Flores's way of describing its flows contributes to my understanding of his leveling or "horizontal" poetics, because he merged forms once divided between the supposedly "high" and "low" planes of culture. Cuba had a radio station broadcasting classical music around the clock, and Flores told me he followed this station for years. But he was not familiar with a broad range of contemporary classical composers known for their interest in repetition: Philip Glass, yes . . . but who is this Steve Reich person, he asked? Popular music from the Caribbean region was more consistently available to Flores, and he emphasized that repetition is an important component of its Cuban forms. In fact, he said, he sometimes imagined his writing as discography. So while he was very conscious of participating in a prose poetry tradition linked back to the French writers of the nineteenth century, and in concepts translatable to classical music, he was equally interested in comparing each little poem to a "little" song. This perspective caused him to take all the more interest in Alamar's rap and hiphop traditions, and through these popular musical forms Flores circled back to the origins of poetry in song and chant. Thus he described his prose poetry to me as a synthesis of approaches that are often opposed to each other: it is at once experimental and traditional, written and sung, created for the page and for performance.

Paintings and Galleries

During Flores's brief visit to New York to read at the Americas Society in 2011, his only trip outside Cuba to date, we took a few hours to visit the Museum of Modern Art. There he stood before canvases he loves but had only seen as occasional reproductions. Flores was particularly moved by the paintings of Vassily Kandinsky. He stopped our group to point out one in particular, saying that for twenty years he had kept a poster of that canvas on the wall of his family's Alamar apartment.

This anecdote opens out into *The Counterpunch*: the book is divided into a set of galleries. In the original Spanish version of the book, their designation as "PeaNut Galleries" appears in English. For English speakers, the reference to a peanut gallery may work a bit differently than it does for the Spanish-language readers, yet in ways that I still find relevant: it may first invoke the idea of social margins, a group located on the edge of the action rather than at its center. The opinions of people in the peanut gallery may or may not be taken seriously, no matter how loudly that group may speak out. This understanding of the peanut gallery complements some of the book's content, particularly the leveling humor important to Flores's "horizontal" philosophy.

However, the *art* gallery is more central to the writer's aesthetic and organization of the book as a whole. While developing the shape of this manuscript, Flores said, he specifically imagined museum galleries. Poems in which Flores highlights a single color (such as red in "The blender") or geometric quality (the slope in "The messenger") draw energy from visual fields. Why the addition of the "PeaNut" to the Spanish? The peanut, he explained to me, is diminutive. Its very small size "conveys the minimalist feel of the writing" ("anuncia el sentido minimalista de la escritura"). For those familiar with the history of prose poetry, such as French examples, it will not be surprising to see this connection to the visual arts.

Beyond Flores's personal enjoyment of Baudelaire's "little poems in prose," minimalism took on special meaning for him when he began composing this book. At the time he had completed his previous collection, *Los pájaros escritos*, and entered a period of creative crisis. While still unable to write anything he found significant, he encountered music and writing by John Cage. At roughly the same time he got access to catalogues displaying the work of minimalist painters and sculptors. These sources, and the music of Philip Glass, left a deep impact on his thoughts about composition. The transformation he experienced "will be definitive until the last of all [his] days," Flores told me ("será definitivo hasta el último día entre [sus] días").

Minimalism felt natural to him, organic. It ran counter to the grain of a historically important literary tradition on the island, the baroque aesthetic, with its emphasis on excess. I would pause here to note that scholars have identified an important strain of cultural pluralism in works derived from the baroque, one that arguably relates well to many aspects of Flores's work, so I don't want to dismiss potential connections to be made there. But this observation need not negate the value of situating his minimalist poetics in respectful artistic contrast to what he calls the "majestic" tradition of the baroque, its legacies famously demonstrated in recent island poetry by José Lezama Lima—the very poet in whose historic home Flores attended his first writing workshops at the age of twenty.

The discipline required to work in very small forms allows Flores to conjure particular fields of energy. If a gallery can contain art, another fundamental point is that the gallery is an enclosed space. Evoking confinement generates a desire to break through boundaries and imagine greater freedoms, a tension historically associated with prose poetry. In work following Baudelaire's exploration of the genre, for example, "many pieces end either with the desire to flee the composed scene or despair at the impossibility of such escape" (Murphy 18). Flores and López remarked on two specific angles emerging from that general sense of confinement in *The Counterpunch*. First, they stated that there's a level on which the book is laid out as a sort of jail, a panopticon: each gallery operates as a cell shared by a particular group. The first and last poems in the book, standing alone outside the galleries, function as "solitary confinements" for the poet. Second, they noted that museums operate rather like mausoleums. Museums are spaces for preserving artifacts of the dead. "A necrophiliac strain runs throughout the entire book," Flores observed ("Hay una sustancia necrófila que recorre todo el libro"), and it surfaces in a gallery devoted to the dead.

The most obvious structural feature uniting the poems of *The Counterpunch* across the galleries is repetition, which allows for a spectrum of effects. The heads and tails of many small pieces acquire their shapes from repetitive techniques: Flores employs anaphora, the repetition of beginnings; and he revisits repetition to create endings, offering closure through variations on preceding lines. Inspired by Valery's notes on seashells, Flores thinks of his structures as circles and spirals. Rodríguez argues that Flores goes beyond using repetition as a formal technique. She makes the provocative suggestion that Flores's "repetition becomes his primary metaphor" ("repetir se convierte en su metáfora primordial"). It also enables a meditative reading experience, a flow in which repetition allows for the appreciation of incremental differences as a poem plays out: in the workings of these rhythms, I find a wonderful dialogue between Flores and another one of France's great prose poets, René Char. I leave it to readers to continue exploring a question—perhaps the major question—that arises for this book: how might repetition-as-metaphor relate to the mission Flores has described for his trilogy, "the poetical resurrection of Alamar"?

Lastly, much prose by poets emphasizes personal experience and subjective knowledge while also tapping into social spheres and flirting with claims to objectivity. I therefore return to the doubleness I propose earlier in this introduction. The poetry, situated along the borderlines between public and private experience, allows for interplays between different types of knowledge.

It is this quality that best opens up the possibility of reading *The Counterpunch* as counter-discourse, in the tradition of the prose poem: Flores deploys a set of strategies enabling a poetic response to discourse patterns dominant in the writer's community, ideally allowing the writer to subvert those patterns (Murphy 5). Flores certainly hints at this possibility in the title to his book. In boxing, a counterpunch is a response to an opponent's attack. More specifically, it takes advantage of the attacker's move: the counterpunch represents an effort to exploit a space newly opened by the movements of your opponent.

Notes: Inside the Galleries

Details regarding occupants of the PeaNut Galleries appear in short sketches below. Some of these details have affected my translations. I include others for English-language readers who may have no other way to suss out some of Flores's cultural and/or local references, even if they understand other aspects of a poem.

The cast of memorable characters dotting the Alamar landscape is inspired in part by residents of the neighborhood, as well as by writers from greater Havana. Whatever their "original" status, all of them have been subjected to the writer's reconfigurations—his particular uses of estrangement, out of which the irreality of his Alamar develops. For this reason Flores was reluctant to identify many figures in his poems as individuals: where real people served as prompts, he emphasized that their identities and contexts migrated throughout the composition process to meet whatever needs the finished poem finally serves. During that process he added autobiographical elements and the voices of imaginary people, merging self with subject. Due to Flores's creative license, it would be inaccurate to treat the book as straightforward documentation of local society, despite the importance of community.

Rodríguez—who makes one of the more obvious appearances in the book as R.M.R—proposes that all of his characters "live in the 'machi-nation' and their functions correspond to the anthropology of functions, more

than any real action" ("viven en la 'maqui-nación' y sus oficios correspon-
den a la antropología de los oficios, más que a una acción real"). In her
opinion it may be most appropriate to treat these figures as characters in
a tragedy: "The everyday heroes, their anonymous characters, are com-
posed of the two 'hemispheres of being and unbeing'; of rise and fall;
construction and destruction; mobility and stasis" ("Los héroes de cada
día, sus personajes anónimos, están compuestos por los dos 'hemisferios
de ser y no ser'; de elevación y caída; de construcción y destrucción; de
movilidad y fijeza").

Flores does identify the person who inspired his title poem, with
which the book closes: boxer Emilio Correa, who lived in Alamar for more
than twenty years. An Olympic and world welter-weight champion, Cor-
rea fell on hard times and struggled with alcoholism. As he was writing
this poem Flores watched the movie "Hurricane," starring Denzel Wash-
ington, several times. Images of the two boxers merged in his mind. The
hip-hopping sequences are moves Flores gave to these imagined boxers—
and at the same time, they pay respect to the musical form so popular in
recent decades in Alamar.

This is not to say that Flores strives to use only the latest and smooth-
est of tones in his poetry: at several points in our discussions, he request-
ed that I look for moments to insert more awkward and archaic moments
amid the athleticism and punch of his phrasings, in order to evoke the
less than graceful aspects of life as a whole in the translation. The poetry,
he specified, should not be as smooth and pleasing as the music he heard
around him.

Considering that request in retrospect, I now see an implied per-
sona uniting the collection despite its fragmentation and partial use of
distanced (third-person) perspectives. That persona renders tensions be-
tween personal and collective, private and public more ambiguous.

PeaNut Gallery I

The opening poem, "The diver," serves as a sort of manifesto.
The title character refers not to just any sort of diver but to homeless
and destitute people who comb through dumpsters in Alamar; the
"horizontal" shape of properties mentioned in the poem refers to the
standard apartment shape in the many identical buildings compris-
ing the housing community today. It is against the background of
such everyday details that the newly announced alternative cultural

expression will take form. The poems that follow this opener emphasize play. They're influenced by poetry for children, whose images dominate the rest of this gallery. The skater of death is based on a real roller-blader seen frequently in the streets; in the same poem, Rachiel is a child who lived near Flores. This poem is one of several to include invented words and other playful treatments of language. In the gallery as a whole, play expands into sport, spreading into adult worlds. Flores, who loves soccer, conceives of athletes like Roberto Baggio as poets working in other modes. "Bonus sprint" uses humor to link cycling with the Peter Pan brigade, a famous migration of children conflating childhood innocence with daunting adult realities.

PeaNut Gallery II

Women's gallery. Includes a poem, "The kiss," dedicated to the writer's mother. Another, "My girl," is for Mayra López: Flores and López associated the poem with a classic, romantic song by the same name, performed by the late José Antonio Méndez. "R.M.R" evokes poet Reina María Rodríguez (though Flores added that the initials R.M.R may call up Rilke). Details about her daily life are embedded in the poem: Rodríguez lives on the top of a building with no elevator, so one must march up and down the stairs for visits; and one of her four children is named Edgar. Flores reflected that while there are many poems dedicated to mothers in Cuban literature, there are few like this one dedicated to literary godmother figures; he mused that there's probably some psychoanalytic angle involved. Remaining portraits in this gallery deal with women alienated in some way. Some are prisoners in the jail at El Cacahual. Some are prostitutes. Margot the plump: lover of Francois Villon. "Miss Boyero" refers to a different form of alienation and enclosure: Boyero is the name of a street housing a psychiatric hospital, from which the poem's protagonist escapes. "The columbine," also dealing with medical contexts, emerges loosely from Flores's discussions with a friend who served as a translator for the doctor Patch Adams. Adams is known for bringing humor to his work with patients, and for his dedication to bringing care to those with little access to expensive medical resources. Flores recalled extended conversations about the dignity of people with Down syndrome.

PeaNut Gallery III

Gallery of the dead. Flores wondered whether the poems might be read as elegies in miniature. "At the scene of the crime" was inspired by memories shared by a doctor who served in the Cuban military in Africa in the 1980s. "The crane" includes one of the moments of deliberately archaic and thus awkward speech that Flores asked me to add to the translation as a whole: "meat comes dear" is not a strictly literal rendition but conveys my fidelity to the poet's larger vision, which imagines a lyrical subject who *really needs* renewal and resurrection in Alamar. I scattered similar moments elsewhere in the book after becoming aware of the implied speaker who, perhaps, gives a form of unity to the book across its miniature parts. "D-32" also refers to memories from the 1980s, in this case the end of that decade, as economic crisis intensified in Cuba and political dissent was on the rise. We discussed the currencies in play in "The smith," so my rendition is directly influenced by Flores's remarks on the famously unequal relations between dollars and the Cuban peso—that is, it's a contextual rather than literal translation. The Selena with which the deceased "Selena-ist" has bonded is a Soviet-produced radio from many decades ago: Flores said that this personage is listening for news broadcasts from abroad. (He himself still had a Selena radio.) Flores's favorite poem in the book appears in this section: "The excavator in the mine."

PeaNut Gallery IV

Poems originally inspired by Cuban writers, most from Havana. "The leper": refers to a friend of the author who is gay. Depicted as villains of an imaginary, fairytale world, the "driller" characters are those who have persecuted the friend for his sexuality, blocking opportunities and creative expression. But he survives. For Flores, this poem is central to his vision of creative "resurrection" in Alamar, and its singsong motion provides an aesthetic connection to the first gallery. The final poem of this gallery, "Train to Vegas," refers to Flores's performance CD, *Vegas Town*: he called it a flight from a suburban imaginary to the rural imaginary.

PeaNut Gallery V

Opens with a self-portrait, "The lizard." The remaining pieces unfold in chronological succession, running from John Keats and his romanticism through "Man on sofa," first inspired by the Austrian poet Ernest Händel. In addition to writers openly named in the poems, some others making appearances include Friedrich Hölderlin, Constantine P. Cavafy, and Thomas Merton (who appears in the poem addressing doctor/poet/friend Pedro Marqués de Armas). The picturesque German specialists spoke at "La azotea de Reina," the name by which informal gatherings of writers at Rodríguez's rooftop home overlooking Ánimas street are known. "This gallery can be seen as the cells designated for foreigners in Cuban jails," Flores said ("Esta galería puede verse como esas celdas para extranjeros que hay en las cárceles cubanas").

A final painting of note. Flores asserts that he is actually descended from the famous Cuban bandit Manuel García, just as his poem "Borges spankspank" claims. The relation is on the side of his mother, Hilda Flores García. You can see a portrait of the historical bandit on display at Havana's Museum of Fine Arts in the Cuban Division.

Kristin Dykstra

Endnotes

1. There were a variety of emails between Flores and myself over the course of a couple of years as I finished the book, ranging from July 2010 through September 2012. In addition, I took notes from personal conversations with Flores while visiting his home in Alamar on June 10, 2010, and later on May 19 and 20, 2011.

2. For an introduction to audio, video, and commentary focused on this aspect of Flores's poetry, see the May 2015 feature on Flores at Mónica's "Legibles" area in http://www.cuba counterpoints.com/legibles/in-legibles-three-poems-by-juan-carlos-flores/#more-774

3. Two commentaries that I wrote earlier in the translation process offer complementary information. "Finding A Way in Alamar" discusses the built environment as well as poetry by Juan Carlos Flores and his late friend Ángel Escobar (see *Review: Literature and Arts of the Americas* 82, "Cuba Inside and Out," 44.1, May 2011, 29–38). An earlier writeup and translations appeared in *La Habana Elegante*; the *LHE* feature includes photographs from Flores's home amongst its illustrations (see "On Poetical Renovations in Alamar," Fall/Winter 2010, in "La azotea de Reina": <http://www.habanaelegante.com/Fall_Winter_2010/Azotea_DykstraFlores.html>)

4. See http://www.youtube.com/watch?v=cKbjdJ3Ar-U for the trailer; Emilio Vega is credited in some places but not all with working on the music with Carreras. For individual poem audio from this Flores book, http://www.goear.com/listen/2095483/pequeno-caliban-juan-carlos-flores is a direct link to "Pequeño caliban," or "Little caliban," from which additional poems can be located. The much longer video on the making of the DVD, with English sub-

titles, appears at http://www.youtube.com/watch?v=UxA7Cacr4FI. See also Mónica's 2015 overview about resources posted at *Cuba Counterpoint*, previously noted.

5. The magazine *La Habana Elegante* published one of these photographs in a feature about Flores, available at http://www.habanaelegante.com/Fall_Winter_2010/Azotea_Dykstra Flores.html.

Works Cited

Birkenmaier, Anke, and Esther Whitfield, eds. *Havana Beyond the Ruins: Cultural Mappings after 1989*. Durham, NC: Duke University Press, 2011.

Fernandes, Sujatha. "Made in Havana City: Rap Music, Space, and Racial Politics." In Birkenmaier and Whitfield, 173–186.

Flores, Juan Carlos. *El contragolpe (y otros poemas horizontales)*. Havana: Editorial Letras Cubanas, 2009.

Murphy, Margueritte. *A Tradition of Subversion: The Prose Poem in English from Wilde to Ashbery*. Amherst, MA: University of Massachusetts Press, 1992.

Rodríguez, Reina María. "Almagra viva." *La Habana Elegante, Segunda Época* (Spring–Summer 2006). Digital: http://www.habanaelegante.com/SpringSummer2006/AzoteaDos .html

Scarpaci, Joseph, Roberto Segre, and Mario Coyula. *Havana: Two Faces of the Antillean Metropolis*. Revised edition. Chapel Hill, NC: University of North Carolina Press, 2002.

Spaar, Lisa Russ. "An Interview with Hank Lazer." *The Chronicle of Higher Education* (June 2, 2011). Digital: http://chronicle.com/blogs/arts/an-interview-with-hank-lazer/29495

The Counterpunch (and Other Horizontal Poems)
El contragolpe (y otros poemas horizontales)

Photograph of Juan Carlos Flores in Havana's Fine Arts Museum (Cuban division) in January 2013; courtesy of Kristin Dykstra

OPENING

Manuscritos

Descifrar lo que está escrito en el viento, es tarea difícil, detrás de la cerca o cortina metálica, humo, quienes no se aventuraban a saltar, se dedicaban a un parloteo de vecinos, sobre lo que había y se hacía detrás de la cerca o cortina metálica, quienes se aventuraban a saltar, regresaban callados, como si hubiesen contraído una enfermedad que les impidiese el habla, detrás de la cerca o cortina metálica, humo, escribir lo que está cifrado en el viento, es tarea difícil.

Manuscripts

Deciphering what's written in the wind, it's a difficult task, behind the metallic fence or curtain, smoke, those who didn't risk the leap, they devoted themselves to neighborly chatter, about what was there and what was done behind the metallic fence or curtain, those who risked the leap, they came back quieted, as if they had contracted some illness that impeded their speech, behind the metallic fence or curtain, smoke, writing what's encrypted in the wind, it's a difficult task.

PeaNut Gallery I

El buzo

Sea El buzo, ocupación que se ejerce o propiedad horizontal o hijo bobo de patria o niño con biberón (áreas densas de pasto, hay los terrenos baldíos, donde el vecindario peatonal arroja los escombros de sus vidas y entre la mala hierba crece la seta de una nueva civilidad, sin incluirse aún en mapas de la contracultura), sea El buzo, ocupación que se ejerce o propiedad horizontal o hijo bobo de patria o niño con biberón (áreas densas de pasto, hay los terrenos baldíos, donde el vecindario peatonal arroja los escombros de sus vidas y entre la mala hierba crece la seta de una nueva civilidad, sin incluirse aún en mapas de la contracultura), sea El buzo, ocupación que se ejerce o propiedad horizontal o hijo bobo de patria o niño con biberón: "a la hora señalada, cuando me llamen por mi nombre, no responderé".

The diver

Whether The dumpster diver be occupation one exercises or horizontal
real estate or foolish son of the homeland or child feeding from bottle
(areas thick with grass, there are unused wastelands, where pedestrians
from the neighborhood throw debris from their daily lives and among
weeds, the first mushroom rises for a new civility, not yet included on
maps of the counterculture), whether The diver be occupation one ex-
ercises or horizontal real estate or foolish son of the homeland or child
feeding from bottle (areas thick with grass, there are unused wastelands,
where pedestrians from the neighborhood throw debris from their daily
lives and among weeds, the first mushroom rises for a new civility, not
yet included on maps of the counterculture), whether The diver be occu-
pation one exercises, horizontal real estate, foolish son of the homeland,
or child feeding from bottle: "at the appointed hour, when they call me
by my name, I will not respond."

Pequeño caliban

El patinador de la muerte cruza veloz por la avenida, entre los autos y los transeúntes, al patinador de la muerte o al patinamuer de la dor hoy sólo quiero mirar, ojos de puerco jíbaro, hay un niño que mira, hay un niño cuyo nombre es Rachiel. El patinador de la muerte cruza veloz por la avenida, entre los autos y los transeúntes, al patinador de la muerte o al patinamuer de la dor hoy sólo quiero mirar, ojos de puerco jíbaro, hay un niño que mira, hay un niño cuyo nombre es Rachiel. El patinador de la muerte cruza veloz por la avenida, entre los autos y los transeúntes, al patinador de la muerte o al patinamuer de la dor hoy sólo quiero escribir, ojos de puerco jíbaro, hay un niño que escribe, hay un niño cuyo nombre es ya nadie.

Little caliban

The skater of death flies across the avenue, between the cars and the
passersby, today I just want to look, at the skater of death or the skate-
death of door, rustic pig's eyes, there's a boy looking, there's a boy whose
name is Rachiel. The skater of death flies across the avenue, between the
cars and the passersby, today I just want to look, at the skater of death or
the skatedeath of door, rustic pig's eyes, there's a boy looking, there's a
boy whose name is Rachiel. The skater of death flies across the avenue,
between the cars and the passersby, today I just want to write, at the
skater of death or the skatedeath of door, rustic pig's eyes, there's a boy
writing, there's a boy whose name now is nobody.

Meta volante

Ninguna parábola me gusta más que la parábola del segador, mi cabeza
es un aspa, mi cabeza es un aspa, mi cabeza ha usurpado la función de
mis pies, ¿aún queda hierba en el césped?

En esa caravana me hubiera gustado a mí enrolarme, ir tocando
harmónica hasta los fuegos verdes de Jerusalén.

Ninguna parábola me gusta más que la parábola del segador, mi cabeza
es un aspa, mi cabeza es un aspa, mi cabeza ha usurpado la función de
mis pies, ¿aún queda hierba en el césped?

En esa caravana me hubiera gustado a mí enrolarme, ir tocando
harmónica hasta los fuegos verdes de Miami Beach.

Nana, para festejar, a la vuelta de todo, si es que hay vuelta de todo,
guárdame otra bolsa de plástico.

Bonus sprint

No parable gives me more pleasure than the reaper's parable, my head is
a fanblade, my head is a fanblade, my head has usurped the function of
my feet, is any grass left on the field?

I would have liked to join that caravan, playing harmonica all the way to
the green fires of Jerusalem.

No parable gives me more pleasure than the reaper's parable, my head is
a fanblade, my head is a fanblade, my head has usurped the function of
my feet, is any grass left on the field?

I would have liked to join that caravan, playing harmonica all the way to
the green fires of Miami Beach.

Nana, to celebrate, on the other side of it all, if there is another side to it
all, save me another plastic bag.

Visto desde el suelo

Amanece y están en la montaña, respirar otro aire y están en la montaña, gozar es mejor que sufrir y están en la montaña, jugar es mejor que matar y están en la montaña, ex civilistas, lastre abajo, atraviesan la ley, buscando algún tubo de escape.

Seen from the floor

Sun rises and there they are on the mountain, inhaling a different
breeze and they're on the mountain, enjoyment is better than suffering
and they're on the mountain, amusement is better than killing and
they're on the mountain, ex-responsible citizens, ballast dropped, climb-
ing across the law, in search of some chute for escape.

Fuchi

Fría está la mañana, la película de niebla hace que se confundan iglesias y bares. Fuchi, simplemente, sostener, con todo el cuerpo, en el aire una pelota, más pequeña que un puño, hecha de hilo y semillas. Fría está la mañana y poco abriga el gabán. Sólo hoteles, he construido edificios en los que nadie, nunca ha de habitar. Fría está la mañana, la película de niebla hace que se confundan iglesias y bares. Aquel que tuvo la vana alegría de mujer o gallina ponedora, mientras colocaba ladrillos, mira hoy hacia el círculo dorado donde se colocan los seis jugadores que, sin proponérselo, traspasaron la cerca de púas que divide al occidente, del oriente, al futuro, del pasado. Aunque el sol ya salió, fría está aún la mañana y poco abriga el gabán. Compañero, ¿no habrá por ahí un bar abierto, en el que pueda tomarme una poca de ron?

Hacky sack

Cold is the morning, the film of fog causes confusion of churches with bars. Hacky sack, simply keeping a ball up in the air, using the entire body, the ball smaller than a fist, made of string and seeds. Cold is the morning and the jacket, not so warm. Just hotels, I've constructed buildings in which no one, ever, has to live. Cold is the morning, the film of fog causes confusion of churches with bars. Today the guy who felt the vain happiness of a woman or laying hen, while he was laying bricks, looks toward the golden circle, into which six players have moved, unintentionally, they've gone through the fence of thorns dividing the west from the east, the future from the past. Though the sun is up already, the morning is still cold and the jacket, not so warm. Comrade, isn't there some bar open around here, where I can get a spot of rum?

Mea culpa por Tomás

Tomás, niño venido de la Unión Soviética, a quien nosotros llamábamos
"cabeza de bolo". Porque se alimentaba mejor que nosotros, a golpear
a "cabeza de bolo", porque se vestía mejor que nosotros, a golpear a
"cabeza de bolo", porque tenía mejores juguetes que nosotros, a golpear a
"cabeza de bolo", porque sacaba mejores notas que nosotros, a golpear a
"cabeza de bolo", para que ninguna niña lo mirase, a golpear a "cabeza de
bolo". Creo que frente a Tomás, todos nos sentíamos un poco checos.

Mea culpa for Tomás

Tomás, kid from the Soviet Union, whom we called "bowling-pin head."
Because he ate better than we did, let's smack "bowling-pin head," be-
cause he dressed better than we did, smack "bowling-pin head," because
he had better toys than we did, smack "bowling-pin head," because he
got better grades than we did, smack "bowling-pin head," so no girl
would look at him, smack "bowling-pin head." Next to Tomás I think we
all felt a little bit Czech.

Hay que ver

Mi maestro de kung fu es un hombre que proviene del continente africano.

Sé, por haber indagado, que los estudiantes de kung fu gustan de tener un maestro que provenga de la China dinástica, pero mi maestro de kung fu es un hombre que proviene del continente africano.

Porque no estamos en China, ni siquiera en uno entre los tantos barrios chinos de América, sino en Alamar, lugar de las mixturas, donde estas cosas pasan.

Hay que verlo.

Mi maestro de kung fu es un hombre que profesa la doctrina de Cristo.

Sé, por haber indagado, que los estudiantes de kung fu gustan de tener un maestro que profese la doctrina de Buda, pero mi maestro de kung fu es un hombre que profesa la doctrina de Cristo.

Porque no estamos en China, ni siquiera en uno entre los tantos barrios chinos de América, sino en Alamar, lugar de las mixturas, donde estas cosas pasan.

Hay que verlo.

You have to see

My kung fu master is a man who comes from the African continent.

I know, from having inquired, that students of kung fu like to have a master who comes from dynastic China, but my kung fu master is a man who comes from the African continent.

Because we're not in China, or even in one of the many Chinatowns of the Americas, but in Alamar, site of intermingling, where these things happen.

You have to see him.

My kung fu master is a man who professes the doctrine of Christ.

I know, from having inquired, that students of kung fu like to have a master who professes the doctrine of Buddha, but my kung fu master is a man who professes the doctrine of Christ.

Because we're not in China, or even in one of the many Chinatowns of the Americas, but in Alamar, site of intermingling, where these things happen.

You have to see him.

The band

Tanta gente pasando, y aún recuerdo a los estudiantes del África negra que vivieron en Alamar.

(Ellos me dejaron el amor por el balompié callejero y el amor por las canciones de Bob Marley, dos entre puntales que sostienen mi vida, la vida de quien después de haber girado en U, caminó más allá de la edad que les señalaron los ya viejos maestros.)

Tanta gente pasando, y aún recuerdo a los estudiantes del África negra que vivieron en Alamar.

The band

So many people passing through, and still I remember the students
from black Africa who once lived in Alamar.

(They left me the love for street soccer and the love for Bob Marley's
songs, two of the props holding up my life, the life of a man who, after
making a U-turn, walked past the age predicted by the already aged
teachers.)

So many people passing through, and still I remember the students
from black Africa who once lived in Alamar.

Lucha grecorromana

No menos digno de oda o escultura que un griego.

(Cuando le recordé sus hazañas a aquel hombre rudo, imbatible en el círculo, que a tantos contendientes las espaldas pegó, se le saltaron dos lágrimas, como si fuese un niño.)

No menos digno de oda o escultura que un griego, trabajando en oficio común, por paga miserable y condenado a robar.

Greco-Roman wrestling

No less worthy of ode or sculpture than a Greek.

(When I retold his great achievements to that rough man, unbeatable
in the circle, the man who slammed so many contenders on their backs,
two great tears started from him, as from a child.)

No less worthy of ode or sculpture than a Greek, working at an ordinary
trade, for miserable pay and condemned to stealing.

Carreras de maratón

El corredor de largas distancias, en hora de maitines y blasfemias gástricas, atraviesa avenidas y calles más pequeñas de la parroquia (aristocrática es la soledad, aunque la desconfianza hacia el otro engendra inquisidores), hay un corredor de largas distancias que, en hora de maitines y blasfemias gástricas, atraviesa avenidas y calles más pequeñas de la parroquia (aristocrática es la soledad, aunque la desconfianza hacia el otro engendra inquisidores), ni una bestia ni un dios, un hombre y está solo por el placer de estar solo.

Marathons

The long-distance runner, at the hour for matins and gastric blasphe-
mies, traverses tiniest streets and avenues in the parish (aristocratic is
his solitude, though distrust of the other engenders inquisitors), there's
a long-distance runner who, at the hour for matins and gastric blasphe-
mies, traverses tiniest streets and avenues in the parish (aristocratic is
his solitude, though distrust of the other engenders inquisitors), not a
beast or a god, a man, and alone for the pleasure of being alone.

Mancha, papel y lápiz

Peces voladores (entran y salen del agua, sus movimientos tienen la misma precisión que los movimientos de los atletas clavadistas, mi padre, siendo yo niño, a estos lugares me traía para que aprendiese a leer en el libro de los signos del mundo), peces voladores (entran y salen del agua, sus movimientos tienen la misma precisión que los movimientos de los atletas clavadistas, mi padre, siendo yo niño, a estos lugares me traía para que aprendiese a leer en el libro de los signos del mundo), detrás de cada pez volador la barracuda, hambrienta, puede estar: ¡Y está!

Spot, paper and pen

Flying fish (leap in and out of the water, their movements have the same precision as movements of competitive divers, my father, when I was a child, took me to these places so I would learn to read the book of signs from the world), flying fish (leap in and out of the water, their movements have the same precision as movements of competitive divers, my father, when I was a child, took me to these places so I would learn to read the book of signs from the world), following any flying fish the barracuda, starving, may appear: there!

Zigzag

La sonrisa de una discreta dama de provincia/ la sonrisa de una discreta dama de provincia/ la sonrisa de una discreta dama de provincia, la sonrisa, captada por el adelantado, su ojo a las minúsculas liebres de lo transitorio: "¿Por qué se rie David Tresegué, el delantero jovial, después de haber intentado uno y otro remate, sin haber podido insertar el balón en la red?"

Diversos goleadores, los llamados crak, cuando fallan, hincan las rodillas contra el césped, y apretadas las manos a cada costado de las cabezas, miran hacia el cielo como si allí esperase, sentada, la respuesta a la pregunta que raspa: ustedes, viviendo entre gestos violentos, deberían quizás sonreír: diversos goleadores, los llamados crak, cuando fallan, hincan las rodillas contra el césped, y apretadas las manos a cada costado de las cabezas, miran hacia el cielo como si allí esperase, sentada, la respuesta a la pregunta que raspa.

La sonrisa de una discreta dama de provincia/ la sonrisa de una discreta dama de provincia/ la sonrisa de una discreta dama de provincia, la sonrisa, captada por el adelantado, su ojo a las minúsculas liebres de lo transitorio: "¿Por qué se ríe David Tresegué, el delantero jovial, después de haber intentado uno y otro remate, sin haber podido insertar el balón en la red?"

Zigzag

The smile of a discreet lady from the countryside / smile of a discreet lady from the countryside / smile of a discreet lady from the countryside, the smile, captured by the forward, his eye on fugacity's tiniest fleet hares: "Why does he smile, David Trezeguet, the jolly striker, having tried one shot after another, without getting the ball in the net?"

Many goal scorers, the ones called crack shots, when they miss, fall to their knees on the pitch, hands pressed to the sides of their heads, and look up toward the sky as if the answer sat there waiting, the answer to the question that wounds: all of you, living between violent gestures, maybe you should smile: many goal scorers, the ones called crack shots, when they miss, fall to their knees on the pitch, hands pressed to the sides of their heads, and look up toward the sky as if the answer sat there waiting, the answer to the question that wounds.

The smile of a discreet lady from the countryside / smile of a discreet lady from the countryside / smile of a discreet lady from the countryside, the smile, captured by the forward, his eye on fugacity's tiniest fleet hares: "Why does he smile, David Trezeguet, the jolly striker, having tried one shot after another, without getting the ball in the net?"

El número 10

Roberto Baggio está frente al portero, si inserta el balón en la red, su equipo Italia podrá ganar la codiciada, la áurea copa, yo, una y mil sombras acompasadamente ardiendo, que finalmente me ordené, en orden del Sutra del Loto, sé lo que significa pertenecer a un equipo de fútbol, sé lo que significa acertar y sé lo que significa fallar, arte o fútbol o guerra, trabajar por algo cansa, trabajar por nada cansa más. Roberto Baggio está frente al portero, si inserta el balón en la red, su equipo Italia podrá ganar la codiciada, la áurea copa, pero Roberto Baggio falla, yo, una y mil sombras acompasadamente ardiendo, que finalmente me ordené, en orden del Sutra del Loto, sé lo que significa pertenecer a un equipo de fútbol, sé lo que significa acertar y sé lo que significa fallar, arte o fútbol o guerra, trabajar por algo cansa, trabajar por nada cansa más: aquellas nanas, mi madre, aquellas nanas, cántame una.

Number 10

Roberto Baggio is in front of the goalie, if he puts the ball in the net, his Team Italy will be able to win the coveted, the golden cup, I, a thousand and one shadows rhythmically burning, at last I put my things in order, within the order of the Lotus Sutra, I know what it means to belong to a soccer team, I know what it means to nail it and what it means to miss, art or soccer or war, working for something wears you out, working for nothing wears you out more. Roberto Baggio is in front of the goalie, if he puts the ball in the net, his Team Italy will be able to win the coveted, the golden cup, but Roberto Baggio misses, I, a thousand and one shadows rhythmically burning, at last I put my things in order, within the order of the Lotus Sutra, I know what it means to belong to a soccer team, I know what it means to nail it and what it means to miss, art or soccer or war, working for something wears you out, working for nothing wears you out more: those lullabies, mother, those lullabies, sing one for me.

Parque de diversiones

Los niños, si se aburren, rompen cuanto cristal encuentran. El mendigo, sobre periódicos echado, en noches de cuaresma, cara hacia bodega celeste, soñó el parque. Ahora, con aparatos viejos, extraídos de otro parque, están construyendo el parque. Si me aburro, rompo cuanto cristal encuentro, yo necesito un parque.

Amusement park

Kids, if they get bored, break all the glass they find. The beggar, sprawled on newspapers, during the nights of Lent, face to the celestial store, dreams up the park. Now with aging apparatus, parts extracted from another park, they're building the park. If I get bored I break all the glass I find, I need a park.

PeaNut Gallery II

El beso

Larga la noche y frente a las puertas rojas del amanecer me digo: si yo tuviera entre mis manos la guitarra, no sería: Silvio Rodríguez, ni Chico Buarque, ni Bob Dylan, ni Bob Marley. Ni trova, ni zamba, ni blues, ni reggae. Ni Cuba, ni Brasil, ni Estados Unidos, ni Jamaica. Sería un hombre anónimo y remoto, de un lugar anónimo y remoto, cantando una canción anónima y remota. Madre, te necesito, madre, te amo, creo que jamás podré aprender a acordonarme los zapatos.

The kiss

Long is the night and at dawn's crimson gates I say to myself: if I had a guitar between my hands, I wouldn't be Silvio Rodríguez, or Chico Buarque, or Bob Dylan, or Bob Marley. Not ballad, or zamba, or blues, or reggae. Not Cuba, or Brazil, or the US, or Jamaica. I would be a remote and anonymous man, from a remote and anonymous place, singing a remote and anonymous song. Mother, I need you, mother, I love you, I don't think I'll ever learn how to lace my own shoes.

La sibila

Máquina de coser Singer, un regalo de bodas, lo mismo que una
carretilla roja, o ciudad que se edifica piedra sobre piedra, muerte sobre
muerte, medio siglo después, la casada perfecta, otra anciana combada,
mueve y mueve el pedal.

The sibyl

Singer sewing machine, a wedding present, same as a red wheelbarrow, or city erected one stone on top of another, one death on top of another, half a century later, the perfect wife, another sagging elderly lady, she pumps and pumps the pedal.

Una puta en el malecón | La misma puta en el Cacahual

Trabajar cansa, eso según. Cada vez hay menos putas trabajando en el malecón y cada vez hay más putas trabajando en la cárcel de putas. Cuando ellas son las montadas, aquí a las putas las llaman jineteras, una entre tantas máscaras lingüísticas hechas para disfrazar la brutalidad de lo real. ¿Cuántas putas hay trabajando en el malecón?, ¿cuántas putas hay trabajando en la cárcel de putas?, ¿cuánto gana una puta trabajando en el malecón?, ¿cuánto gana una puta trabajando en la cárcel de putas?

A whore at the seawall | Same whore in women's prison

Working wipes you out, this according to. Fewer and fewer whores are working the seawall, and more and more whores are working in the women's prison. Here when they're on the bottom, we call whores riders, one of many linguistic masks for disguising the brutality of the real. How many whores are there, working the malecón? How many whores are there, working in the women's prison? How much does a whore earn working the malecón? How much does a whore earn working in the women's prison?

Miss Boyero

Escribo, la paciente o la dama, con abrigo de armiño, a la hora en que las calles reverberan, se pasea por calles laterales, sin importarle el reverbero causal allá arriba, ni los efectos del reverbero causal acá abajo, sobre la pasta cosmética, sucede, la paciente o la dama, con abrigo de armiño, a la hora en que las calles reverberan, se pasea por calles laterales, sin importarle el reverbero causal allá arriba, ni los efectos del reverbero causal acá abajo, sobre la pasta cosmética, escrito para que suceda o sucede para que se escriba, uno de tus prisioneros escapó.

Miss Boyero

I write, the patient or the lady, with ermine coat, at the hour when the streets reverberate, walks through side streets, giving no importance to causal reverberation there above, or to effects of causal reverberation here below, on cosmetic paste, it happens, the patient or the lady, with ermine coat, at the hour when the streets reverberate, walks through side streets, giving no importance to causal reverberation there above, or to effects of causal reverberation here below, on cosmetic paste, written so it might happen or happening so it might be written, one of your prisoners got out.

Ejercicios aeróbicos

Hoy, he amanecido punzón miniaturista y francés, pienso en "Margot la gorda" y en su maestría loada.

Trío de gordas peninsulares, meneando sus caderas, a ritmos de Van Van, gordas, porque su alimento es sancocho, esa flaca playboy, esa, si tiene swing, esa, el dinero sí saca, trio de gordas peninsulares, meneando sus caderas, a ritmos de Van Van, gordas, porque su alimento es sancocho, esa flaca playboy, esa, sí tiene swing, esa, el dinero sí saca, trío de gordas peninsulares, meneando sus caderas, a ritmos de Van Van, gordas, porque su alimento es sancocho, esa flaca playboy, esa, sí tiene swing, esa, el dinero sí saca, timba, la timba.

Hoy, he amanecido punzón miniaturista y francés, pienso en "Margot la gorda" y en su maestría loada.

¡Dios mío, todo lo que hay que hacer para poder conseguir un comprador!

Aerobic exercises

Today I awoke incisive, miniaturist and French, thinking about "Margot the plump" and her glorious skills.

Trio of plump Spanish peninsulars, swinging their hips, to Van Van rhythms, all plump, for their staple is sancocho, the svelte playboy type, that one, yes, she's got swing, that one, the money does bring it out, trio of plump peninsulars, swinging their hips, to Van Van rhythms, all plump, for their staple is sancocho, the svelte playboy type, that one, she's got swing, that one, the money does bring it out, trio of plump peninsulars, swinging their hips, to Van Van rhythms, all plump, for their staple is sancocho, the svelte playboy type, that one, she's got swing, that one, the money does bring it out, timba, the timba.

Today, I awoke incisive, miniaturist and French, thinking about "Margot the plump" and her glorious skills.

My god, all the things you have to do to get a buyer!

El dinosaurio

Yo, pero este yo es otra rodilla astillada, sujeta con fijadores, soy la lectora de novelas rosadas escritas por Corín Tellado. Mi marido reposa, después de un largo día de trabajo en la construcción de odas.

Yo, pero este yo es otra rodilla astillada, sujeta con fijadores, soy la lectora de novelas rosadas escritas por Corín Tellado. Mi marido reposa, después de un largo día de trabajo en la construcción de odas.

Yo, pero este yo es otra rodilla astillada, sujeta con fijadores, soy la lectora de novelas rosadas escritas por Corín Tellado.

The dinosaur

Myself, but this self is another chipped kneecap, held together with
forceps, I'm the reader of sentimental novels written by Corin Tellado.
My husband rests, after a long day at work on the construction of odes.

Myself, but this self is another chipped kneecap, held together with
forceps, I'm the reader of sentimental novels written by Corin Tellado.
My husband rests, after a long day at work on the construction of odes.

Myself, but this self is another chipped kneecap, held together with
forceps, I'm the reader of sentimental novels written by Corin Tellado.

La confederación

Todas las razas.

Mujeres, sobre rocas, con sus trusas llamadas hilos dentales (si no son objetos transitivos, sino seres de aquella deidad descendientes, o por lo menos personas, por qué convirtiendo el territorio en vidriera, van y vienen, meneando pícaramente las dos nalgas, provocando el amontonamiento de ojos). Mujeres, sobre rocas, con sus trusas llamadas hilos dentales.

Todas las razas.

The confederation

Of all races.

Women, on rocks, wearing bottoms known as dental floss (if they're not transitive objects, but beings from that deity descended, or at least people, why go on converting the region into shop windows, they come and go, mischievously wiggling their two cheeks, provoking the pileup of stares). Women, on rocks, wearing bottoms known as dental floss.

Of all races.

Rincón del bolero

Ella canta viejos boleros, la persona insulada, según los dictámenes médicos, está al borde, y si los hombres de la nueva edad de la piedra se acercan, es solamente para descargar sus oscuros paquetes, sin abonar el tributo a la especie, la persona insulada, según los dictámenes médicos, está al borde, y si un bolero pudiese ahuyentar la tristeza, no habría otra boca empapada de alcohol, en la barra, hacia el amanecer, con sucia luz y flores de podrido olor sobre el estiércol del estar, la persona insulada, según los dictámenes médicos, está al borde, ella o alguien, canta viejos boleros.

Bolero corner bar

She's singing old boleros, this isolated person, according to medical files, is on the edge, and if the men of the new stone age approach, it's only to unload their obscure packages, without paying tribute to the sex, this isolated person, according to medical files, is on the edge, and if a bolero could scare off the sadness, there wouldn't be another mouth soused in alcohol, at the bar, around dawn, with dirtied light and flowers smelling rotten over the manure of being there, this isolated person, according to medical files, is on the edge, she or somebody, singing old boleros.

La máquina licuadora

Mujer vestida de rojo, tacones sobre avenida, figura humana contra fondo con césped, o hierbas sin geometrizar (rojo es el color más caliente, en la escala cromática), mujer vestida de rojo, tacones sobre avenida, figura humana contra fondo con césped, o hierbas sin geometrizar (rojo es el color más caliente, en la escala cromática). Mujer vestida de rojo, tacones sobre avenida, figura humana contra fondo con césped, o hierbas sin geometrizar.

The blender

Woman dressed in red, high heels on avenue, human figure against background with grass, or weeds without geometric form (red is the warmest color, on the chromatic scale), woman dressed in red, high heels on avenue, human figure against background with grass, or weeds without geometric form (red is the warmest color, on the chromatic scale). Woman dressed in red, high heels on avenue, human figure against background with grass, or weeds without geometric form.

La palangana

Se me acercó y me dijo: "conozco al subcomandante Marcos, sé que es una buena persona, él y su gente raída, tú deberías escribirle un poema al Zapatismo, revolución espiritual de veras".

En el malecón habanero, muro de las lamentaciones nuestras, soy uno más, insertando su lágrima, pero eso solamente a una mujer interesa y es cubana.

Esta ampolla sí duele y no hay curitas o este líquido corre y no hay tapón.

The washbasin

She came up to me and said: "I know Subcomandante Marcos, I know
he's a good person, he and his worn-down people, you should write a
poem for him about Zapatismo, real spiritual revolution."

At Havana's seafront, our wailing wall, I'm one more guy letting his tear
fall, but that interests only one woman and she is Cuban.

This blister does hurt and there aren't any band-aids or this liquid is
pouring out and there's no plug.

Lavando un viejo pantalón

Nuestras revistas sociales, las revistas picantes, que irritan punta del cohete-lengua, si hay contacto, hipnotista, la truhana, contorsionando, destruye provisionalmente la fealdad de los datos, virtual, la zona para la ingravidez, a nuestros ojos, escalpelos cansados por escudriñar la realidad, roída ya su carne antes de hervir, su hueso más duro que el metal, donde todo, tras su apariencia de camino de seda, tiende a ser fosa común, nuestras revistas sociales, las revistas picantes, que irritan punta del cohete-lengua, si hay contacto, entre uno y otro corsé, van los presos viviendo, mientras se espera amnistía.

Washing an old pair of pants

Our social magazines, racy magazines, which irritate point of the boner-
tongue, if contact is made, hypnotist, the naughty scamp, writhing,
destroys the ugliness of facts for the time being, virtual, the zone for
weightlessness, of our eyes, scalpels worn out by scanning reality, flesh
already eaten away before boiling, bone harder than metal, where
everything, behind its silk road appearance, tends to be a communal
grave, our social magazines, racy magazines, which irritate point of the
boner-tongue, if contact is made, between one corset and another, the
prisoners go on living, while waiting for amnesty.

D-32

Casa, como el interior de un personaje ventrílocuo, con una punzada tragicómica: tiempo muerto de entonces, un pasillo, entre mi espíritu, cojo y los otros espíritus, yo iba a casa de María, la hospedadora, antes de que María, la hospedadora, se convirtiese en Dama primera, de la República en Armas, y fundase un partido político opositor al gobierno centralista y sus tribus caníbales.

(Dicen, esto, no está averiado y sí lo está, esto, no está habaneado y sí lo está.)

D-32

House, like the interior of a celebrity ventriloquist, with a tragicomic pang: dead time leading up to that moment, a hallway, between my spirit, weak, and the other spirits, I was going to María's home, María the host, before María the host would become First lady, of the Provisional Government, before she founded a political party opposing the centralist government and its cannibal tribes.

(They say, this thing, it's not broken down and yes it is, this thing, it's not ha-banned and yes it is.)

R.M.R

Mi madre natural murió, el matador, tres piquetazos, usando una pique-
ta de piquetear cubos de hielo, no sanguínea, otra mujer es mi madre,
mi amor por ella es un amor agápico, yo, que me llamo Juan, sin saber
bien por qué, de vez en vez me llamo Edgar, cocinero, parten dientes los
poemas que escribes, he contestado encogiéndome de hombros, yo subo
una escalera, mi madre natural murió, el matador, tres piquetazos,
usando una piqueta de piquetear cubos de hielo, no sanguínea, otra mujer
es mi madre, mi amor por ella es un amor agápico, yo, que me llamo
Juan, sin saber bien por qué, de vez en vez me llamo Edgar, cocinero,
parten dientes los poemas que escribes, he contestado encogiéndome de
hombros, yo bajo una escalera, madrina, por esta media rota, me entra
Dios, en una pata o en un pie.

R.M.R

My biological mother died, the killer, three jabs, using an icepick for
jabbing cubes of ice, not by blood, another woman is my mother, my
love for her is an agapic love, I, who am called Juan, without really
knowing why, now and then I call myself Edgar, cook, the poems you
write smash teeth, I've answered by shrugging my shoulders, I go up
a stairway, my biological mother died, the killer, three jabs, using an
icepick for jabbing cubes of ice, not by blood, another woman is my
mother, my love for her is an agapic love, I, who am called Juan, without
really knowing why, now and then I call myself Edgar, cook, the poems
you write smash teeth, I've answered by shrugging my shoulders, I go
down a stairway, godmother, through this torn sock, God enters me,
comes in through a paw or a foot.

Novia mía

A fin de cuentas, uno es como esos cines de barrio, que habitualmente ofrecen viejas películas y sólo de vez en vez películas de estreno: casi siempre películas de guerra. ¿Qué pasaría si volviera aquel tiempo en que era como esos cines del centro, que habitualmente ofrecen películas de estreno y sólo de vez en vez viejas películas? Duele saber que pese a todos los afanes uno es como esos cines de barrio, habitualmente ofreciendo viejas películas y sólo de vez en vez películas de estreno: pero hoy, única espectadora en la última fila, estás sentada tú, viendo una película de amor.

My girl

When all is said and done, one resembles those neighborhood theaters, habitually offering old films and only once in a while first-run films: almost always films about war. What would happen if that distant past returned, when one resembled those downtown theaters, habitually offering first-run films and only once in a while old films? It hurts to know that in spite of all intentions one resembles those neighborhood theaters, habitually offering old films and only once in a while first-run films: but today, solitary spectator in the final row, you are seated there, watching a film about love.

La columbina

Babababa. El Síndrome de Down no es enfermedad, estar exento del Síndrome de Down es padecer la enfermedad. Sulamita, mi cabeza, un barquillo en el que echaron cemento, guajirita, mi cabeza, un barquillo en el que echaron cemento, mi cabeza lasqueada, sulamita, mi cabeza lasqueada, guajirita. Hombre, aura regordeta del buen Patch, revendiendo tenis deportivos, suelas y agujeros. Babababa. El Síndrome de Down no es enfermedad, estar exento del Síndrome de Down es padecer la enfermedad. Sulamita, mi cabeza, un barquillo en el que echaron cemento, guajirita, mi cabeza, un barquillo en el que echaron cemento, mi cabeza lasqueada, sulamita, mi cabeza lasqueada, guajirita. Hombre, aura regordeta de buen Patch, revendiendo tenis deportivos, suelas y agujeros. Babababa. El Síndrome de Down no es enfermedad, estar exento del Síndrome de Down es padecer la enfermedad. Sulamita, mi cabeza, un barquillo en el que echaron cemento, guajirita, mi cabeza un barquillo en el que echaron cemento, mi cabeza lasqueada, sulamita, mi cabeza lasqueada, guajirita. Hombre, aura regordeta del buen Patch, revendiendo tenis deportivos, suelas y agujeros. Al individuo a su alcance se dirige: seas tú el nacional o seas tú el extranjero, compra tus tenis deportivos. Te queden grandes o te aprieten, poco importa, compra tus tenis deportivos. Por si vienen rabiosos atomistas, compra tus tenis deportivos. Cava otra vía, topo, al limbo.

(. . . Babababa . . .)

The columbine

Babababa. Down's Syndrome is not an illness, exemption from Down's Syndrome means suffering illness. Sulamita, my head, a boat where they threw on cement, little country girl, my head, a boat where they threw on cement, my flaking head, sulamita, my flaking head, little country girl. A man, chubby aura of the good Patch, reselling athletic shoes, soles and holes. Babababa. Down's Syndrome is not an illness, exemption from Down's Syndrome means suffering illness. Sulamita, my head, a boat where they threw on cement, little country girl, my head, a boat where they threw on cement, my flaking head, sulamita, my flaking head, little country girl. Man, chubby aura of the good Patch, reselling athletic shoes, soles and holes. Babababa. Down's Syndrome is not an illness, exemption from Down's Syndrome means suffering illness. Sulamita, my head, a boat where they threw on cement, little country girl, my head, a boat where they threw on cement, my flaking head, sulamita, my flaking head, little country girl. To the nearest individual he states: whether you're the local or the foreigner, buy yourself athletic shoes. If they're too big or too tight, it doesn't matter much, buy athletic shoes. In case raging nuclear scientists show up, buy athletic shoes. Dig a different tunnel, mole, toward limbo.

(. . . Bababababa . . .)

Los olvidados

"¡Aprisa, bruja peorra, leña para fogata y coles para la sopa, porque pronto vendrán los camaradas!"—dice.

"Si difícil es vivir bajo los puentes, más difícil aún y cansa más vivir encima de los puentes, esta ciudad nunca nos quiso, qué le vamos a hacer"—piensa.

"¡Aprisa, bruja peorra, leña para fogata y coles para la sopa, porque pronto vendrán los camaradas!"—dice.

The forgotten ones

"Faster, nasty witch, wood for the fire and cabbages for soup, because the comrades will get here soon!" he says.

"If it's tough to live under the bridges, it's tougher and more tiring to live on the bridges, this city never wanted us, what can we do," he thinks.

"Faster, nasty witch, wood for the fire and cabbages for soup, because the comrades will get here soon!" he says.

PeaNut Gallery III

La aplanadora

Pasa y por donde pasa queda la superficie lisa (a eso le llaman profilaxis pero podría llamársele también cambio de moneda o canon), pasa y por donde pasa queda la superficie lisa.

The steamroller

It goes by and wherever it goes the surface comes out smooth (they call that prophylaxis but it could be called exchange of currency or canon), it goes by and wherever it goes the surface comes out smooth.

Factorías

Fábricas de lo torcido, porque los gremiales seres torcidos hacen allí sus ritos, echan allí sus fetos, los demonios nacionalistas.

Cómo representar a los gremiales seres torcidos, sin maquillarles, para ocasión de catálogo, si no soy la mandrágora F, ni el ojo distorsionante de la mandrágora F, ni la mano distorsionadora de la mandrágora F, entre torres de hormigón policial, soy el judío, soy el jodido, un bailarín de trompos anarquistas, cuando más.

Fábricas de lo torcido, porque los gremiales seres torcidos hacen allí sus ritos, echan allí sus fetos, los demonios nacionalistas.

"A cada estanco, un aro de niebla alrededor no le vendría mal, pero el pedo caliente, saliendo por las tuberías, le quedaría mejor".

(Derivado de una conversación con José Kózer.)

Foundries

Foundries for contorted things, because professionally contorted beings
practice their rites inside, turn out fetuses there, nationalist demons.

How do you represent the professionally contorted beings, without
applying makeup to them, for the occasion of a catalogue, if I'm not F
the mandrake, or the distorted eye of F the mandrake, or the distorting
hand of F the mandrake, between towers of police concrete, I'm the Jew,
I'm screwed, an anarchist spinning dancer, at most.

Foundries for contorted things, because professionally contorted beings
practice rites there, turn out fetuses there, nationalist demons.

"A hoop of cloud around a tobacconist's would be no bad thing, but a
toasty fart, exiting one's plumbing, would be even better."

(Derived from a conversation with José Kozer.)

Manual de instrucciones

Dale caballo dale, a caballo se le aplica método aerodinámico y caballo caballa, dale caballo dale, a caballo se le aplica método aerodinámico y caballo caballa, dale caballo dale, mas si a caballo se le quita alimento y reposo, el necesario, caballo fallece, antes de.

Instruction manual

Go horse go, with a horse you apply aerodynamic method and horsey horsificates, go horse go, with a horse you apply aerodynamic method and horsey horsificates, go horse go, but if you take away the horse's food and rest, the necessaries, horse croaks, before.

Blanco móvil

Viejo, vuelto loco en la cárcel, traslada una carretilla repleta de excrementos (peso que las piernas le dobla), sé, que tal el revoloteo de una mosca, la escritura molesta, sé que existen herreros de la mente como existen objetos llamados matamoscas, pero la libertad es una, aun entre campos militarizados, viejo, vuelto loco en la cárcel, traslada una carretilla repleta de excrementos (peso que las piernas le dobla), viajante de comercio ilusorio, viaja desde ninguna parte hacia ningún lugar.

Moving target

Old man, gone mad in jail, moves a wheelbarrow full of excrement (weight causing his legs to buckle), I know, like the flutter of a fly, writing annoys, I know blacksmiths of the mind exist just as objects called flyswatters exist, but liberty is one per, though among militarized camps, old man, gone mad in jail, moves a wheelbarrow full of excrement (weight causing his legs to buckle), traveler on illusory business, traveling from no place to nowhere.

José María López Lledín

Le vi recogiendo sobras de comida en tanques de basura, junto a ratas, moscas, perros, no me pareció tener delante plantado a un caballero, menos de París, ni siquiera un clochard, porque París es París y La Habana es La Habana. Hoy le vuelvo a ver, pero a través de un espejo invertido, nuevamente recogiendo sobras de comida en tanques de basura, junto a ratas, moscas, perros, no me parece tener delante plantado a un caballero, menos de París, ni siquiera un clochard, porque París es París y La Habana es La Habana. Han pasado los años y todavía siento vértigo. Primero una ortopedia, después una ascensión. Quienes le convirtieron en mito nacional no le hubieran soportado una semana en sus vidas. Otro viejo asqueroso, un sin familia, tenía nombre civil y pertenecía a un estamento social que crece al derrumbe de las ideologías. Palabras duras para quien tuvo una vida dura.

José María López Lledín

I saw him retrieving leftover food from garbage bins, with the rats, flies, dogs, it didn't look like a gentleman had been introduced there before me, much less one from Paris, or a clochard, because Paris is Paris and Havana Havana. Today I see him again, but through an inverted mirror, again retrieving leftover food from garbage bins, with rats, flies, dogs, it doesn't look like a gentleman has been introduced there before me, much less one from Paris, or a clochard, because Paris is Paris and Havana Havana. The years have passed and I still feel dizzy. First an orthopaedia, then an ascension. Whoever transformed him into a national myth wouldn't have put up with him for a week of their lives. Another disgusting old man, a man without family, he had a fine name and belonged to a social stratum expanding as ideologies collapse. Hard words for one who had a hard life.

El selenita

Nota necrológica, o spot de bailable, o parte del estado real del tiempo,
por lo menos, El hombre del radio receptor, día y noche, con el radio
receptor, junto a la oreja, esperando escuchar la noticia, nota necrológica
o spot de bailable o parte del estado real del tiempo, por lo menos, El
hombre del radio receptor, día y noche, con el radio receptor, junto a la
oreja, esperando escuchar la noticia, nota necrológica, o spot de bailable,
o parte del estado real del tiempo, por lo menos: El hombre del radio
receptor envejeció, enfermó, murió con el radio receptor junto a la oreja.

The Selenaist

Obituary, or spot of dance music, or part of the real state of time, at least,
The radio receiver man, day and night, with the radio receiver, next to
his ear, waiting to hear the news, obituary or a spot of dance music or
part of the real state of time, at least, The radio receiver man, day and
night, with the radio receiver, next to his ear, waiting to hear the news,
the obituary, or a spot of dance music, or part of the real state of time,
at least: The radio receiver man, he aged, he got sick, he died with the
radio receiver next to his ear.

En la escena del crimen

Limpiarse los ojos, ha de tener su lado bueno, aunque pesa demasiado
el hollín de esta época: sintomáticas, salían a calentarse al sol sobre la
carretera asfaltada (los conjuntos, por diversión o por fobia, las mataban,
aplastándolas contra las ruedas de los camiones), limpiarse los ojos, ha de
tener su lado bueno, aunque pesa demasiado el hollín de esta época:
sintomáticas, salían a calentarse al sol sobre la carretera asfaltada (los
conjuntos, por diversión o por fobia, las mataban, aplastándolas contra
las ruedas de los camiones): limpiarse los ojos, ha de tener su lado bueno,
aunque pesa demasiado el hollín de esta época, a mí no me lo crean.

At the scene of the crime

Wipe your eyes, it must have its good side, though the soot of this epoch weighs too heavily: symptomatic, they'd go out to get warm in the sun on the asphalted highway (the bands of soldiers, for their amusement or phobia, would kill them, crushing them under the tires of trucks), wipe your eyes, it must have its good side, though the soot of this epoch weighs too heavily: symptomatic, they'd go out to get warm in the sun on the asphalted highway (the bands of soldiers, for their amusement or phobia, would kill them, crushing them under the tires of trucks): wipe your eyes, it must have its good side, though the soot of this epoch weighs too heavily, none of you should believe me.

La excavadora en la mina

Los mutilados de las guerras del mundo sienten nostalgia por las partes perdidas, al que perdió las piernas, le faltarán para siempre las piernas, al que perdió los brazos, le faltarán para siempre los brazos, al que perdió los ojos, le faltarán para siempre los ojos, al que perdió los dientes, le faltarán para siempre los dientes, cada cual recordando lo que hacía con su parte de menos, al que perdió las piernas, le faltarán para siempre las piernas, al que perdió los brazos, le faltarán para siempre los brazos, al que perdió los ojos, le faltarán para siempre los ojos, al que perdió los dientes, le faltarán para siempre los dientes, y si juntásemos cada parte perdida, haríamos el inventario de la ausencia del hombre.

The excavator in the mine

Those mutilated in the wars of the world feel nostalgia for the lost parts, for the one who lost his legs, his legs will always be missing, for the one who lost his arms, his arms will always be missing, for the one who lost his eyes, his eyes will always be missing, for the one who lost his teeth, his teeth will always be missing, each one remembering what he used to do with the part that's gone, for the one who lost his legs, his legs will always be missing, for the one who lost his arms, his arms will always be missing, for the one who lost his eyes, his eyes will always be missing, for the one who lost his teeth, his teeth will always be missing, and if we put all the lost parts together, it would inventory the absence of man.

¡Bingo!

¿Qué hace ese hombre reventado encima del asfalto, interrumpiendo el tránsito de vehículos y peatones? Colaboracionista, fui pieza perfectamente acoplada al mecanismo social, hasta la mañanita de mi muerte, en que, mientras me afeitaba, comencé a oír voces acusatorias, primero, voces persecutorias, después, y tuve miedo de terminar en la cárcel, así no más. ¿Quién saca a ese hombre reventado de encima del asfalto, para que continúe el tránsito de vehículos y peatones?

Bingo!

What's that mangled body doing on the asphalt, interrupting the flow of vehicles and pedestrians? Collaborator, I was a piece hitched perfectly to society's mechanism, until the very morning of my death, on which, as I was shaving, I started to hear accusatory voices, first, voices of persecution, next, and I got scared of landing in jail, right away. Who will clear his mangled body off the asphalt, so the flow of vehicles and pedestrians can go on?

La grulla

El aguardiente es barato, la carne es cara (algo borracho baila tap encima de los adoquines mojados, restándole importancia al hecho conjetural de una fractura de huesos).

"Joven, hay que mantenerse delgado, en plena forma física, por si se presenta la gran ocasión, pues la fortuna toca solamente una vez a la puerta de casa".

"Joven, hay que mantenerse delgado, en plena forma física, por si se presenta la gran ocasión".

"Joven, hay que mantenerse delgado".

"Joven, hay que mantenerse, en un pie".

El aguardiente es barato, la carne es cara, (algo borracho baila tap encima de los adoquines mojados, restándole importancia al hecho conjetural de una fractura de huesos).

The crane

Some liquor comes cheap, meat comes dear (somewhat drunk he tap-dances over the wet cobblestones, scoring importance from the conjectured case of fractured bone).

"Young man, you have to stay thin, in top physical shape, in case the great opportunity presents itself, well, good fortune knocks just once at the door of a house."

"Young man, you have to stay thin, in top physical shape, in case the great opportunity presents itself.""Young man, you have to stay thin."

"Young man, you have to stay standing, on at least one foot."

Some liquor comes cheap, meat comes dear (somewhat drunk he tap-dances over the wet cobblestones, scoring importance from the conjectured case of fractured bone).

El salvoconducto

Aquel gorila movíase dentro de la funeraria como un portero de hotel, si
no dabas la contraseña y pagabas, a pasar frío en las calles, a exponerte
al peligro nocturno, anti-país necesita anti-poeta de la misma manera
que anti-poeta necesita anti-país, cuando anti-país, narcisísticamente, no
quiere reconocerse en anti-poemas, antipoeta se convierte en enemigo
político, número en una lista, lo peor de todo esto sería que los hijos y los
hijos de los hijos heredaran y ocuparan los oficios, las plazas de los padres.

The safe-conduct

That gorilla was moving around the funeral parlor like the doorman at a hotel, if you didn't say the password or pay up, out with you to the cold of the street, out and exposed to nocturnal dangers, anti-country needs anti-poet in the same way anti-poet needs anti-country, when anti-country, narcissistically, doesn't want to recognize itself in anti-poems, anti-poet transforms into political enemy, number on a list, the worst would be if the children and the children of the children inherited and occupied the trades, the positions of the parents. [1]

El enrejador

Trabajador del metal, a través de otra boca parlera, dice la sagrada boca Ifá, que mi divinidad, la rectora, es Orggún, pero yo digo que es el dólar, cualquier moneda dura.

Aunque conserve algún diente/ un tigre cebado siempre es un tigre esclerótico/ si la clientela no tuviera un miedo atroz al vecindario/ donde no hay ya compañeros/ porque nunca acompañan/ sino los asediantes/ porque asedian/ de cuál modo sustentaría a la prole/ aunque conserve algún diente/ un tigre cebado siempre es un tigre esclerótico/ de poco sirvió la tigritud/

Trabajador del metal, a través de otra boca parlera, dice la sagrada boca Ifá, que mi divinidad, la rectora, es Orggún, pero yo digo que es el dólar, cualquier moneda dura.

The smith

Metalworker, talkative through someone else's mouth, says the sacred mouth Ifá, that my deity, governing spirit, is Orggún, but I say it's the dollar, any currency beating our peso.

Though he may still have teeth / a man-eating tiger is always a sclerotic tiger / if the clientele were not terribly afraid of the vicinity / where there are no longer comrades / because they offer no camaraderie /but to besiege / laying siege / to feed their litters / though he may still have teeth / a man-eating tiger is always a sclerotic tiger / which has been of little benefit to tigritude /

Metalworker, talkative through someone else's mouth, says the sacred mouth Ifá, that my deity, governing spirit, is Orggún, but I say it's the dollar, any currency beating our peso.

El mensajero

Sube, por la pendiente de la mañana, entre minutos que son piedras, trayéndonos noticias del arroz y otras noticias de interés culinario, y otras noticias del país.

Historiador, a su modo, nadie mejor que él descifra la libreta de abastecimientos, cartilla de racionamiento, en época de posguerra, papeles también de notaría.

Baja, por la pendiente de la mañana, entre minutos que son piedras, después de habernos dado noticias del arroz y otras noticias de interés culinario, y otras noticias del país.

The messenger

He ascends the morning's slope, among minutes that are stones,
bringing us news of rice, and other news of culinary interest, and
other news of the nation.

Historian, in his way, no one better than him at deciphering the
passbook for supplies, ration book, in postwar period, notary
papers too.

He descends the morning's slope, among minutes that are stones,
having brought us news of rice, and other news of culinary interest,
and other news of the nation.

El gigante

A los talabarteros, estría, la que deja la aguja en la dermis, estría, a los
enterradores, catre, donde cae cada noche, catre, hasta cuándo el gobierno,
su táctica, su estrategia amorosa, saca del monedero billete, con cara
de Camilo, y lo muestra, a los talabarteros, estría, la que deja la aguja
en la dermis, estría, a los enterradores, catre, donde cae cada noche,
catre, hasta cuándo el gobierno, su táctica, su estrategia amorosa, saca
del monedero billete, con cara de Camilo, y lo muestra, este ladrillo, al
menos, uno, un ladrillazo, al menos.

The giant

To the beltmakers, stretchmark, like needle leaves on dermis, stretch-
mark, to the gravediggers, cot, where each night falls, cot, how long will
the government, its gambit, its amorous strategizing, remove bill from
purse, bill with Camilo's face, and show it, to the beltmakers, stretchmark,
like needle leaves on dermis, stretchmark, to the gravediggers, cot,
where each night falls, cot, how long will the government, its gambit, its
amorous strategizing, remove bill from purse, bill with Camilo's face,
and show it, this brick, at least, one, a volley of bricks, at least.

Zapateo

Toc toc toc toc: El aparato de motor roto y sin continuidad, otro feo cadáver, sobre el jardín de rosas monocromatizadas, meadero para vulgares perros citadinos, a fin de cuentas, donde lo muerto es carne procesal, alimento de lo sagrado, y tras cada banquete engorda el ego grupal de comensales, me pidieron escribiese página obituaria.

Toc toc toc toc: El aparato de motor roto y sin continuidad, otro feo cadáver, sobre el jardín de rosas monocromatizadas, meadero para vulgares perros citadinos, a fin de cuentas, donde lo muerto es carne procesal, alimento de lo sagrado, y tras cada banquete engorda el ego grupal de comensales, me pidieron escribiese página obituaria.

Toc toc toc toc: El aparato de motor roto y sin continuidad, otro feo cadáver, sobre el jardín de rosas monocromatizadas, meadero para vulgares perros citadinos, a fin de cuentas, donde lo muerto es carne procesal, alimento de lo sagrado, y tras cada banquete engorda el ego grupal de comensales, me pidieron escribiese página obituaria.

En vez de la página solicitada, este zapateo sarcástico

Tapdance

Tock tock tock tock: The motor's apparatus broken and discontinuous, another ugly cadaver, on the garden of monochromatized roses, a john for filthy urban dogs, in the end, where that which is dead is decomposing meat, food from the sacred, and after every banquet the collective ego of the diners expands, they asked me to write an obituary page.

Tock tock tock tock: The motor's apparatus broken and discontinuous, another ugly cadaver, over the garden of monochromatized roses, a john for filthy urban dogs, in the end, where that which is dead is decomposing meat, food from the sacred, and after every banquet the collective ego of the diners expands, they asked me to write an obituary page.

Tock tock tock tock: The motor's apparatus broken and discontinuous, another ugly cadaver, over the garden of monochromatized roses, a john for filthy urban dogs, in the end, where that which is dead is decomposing meat, food from the sacred, and after every banquet the collective ego of the diners expands, they asked me to write an obituary page.

> Instead of the page they solicited, this sarcastic tap dance

Maqui-nación

Futura pieza, en almacén de antiguallas o museo arqueológico, hay la-biomáquina-animista. Pesado automóvil gigante, para cumplir hoja de ruta, tiene que continuar extrayéndoles la sangre, como si los donantes fueran el pozo de la sangre, y no esos seres anémicos, seres de piel pegada al hueso, seres lamiendo las marcas de la usura, sin poderse correr hacia un punto de corte, punto sin regresión ni reciclaje posible. Algo que borre definitivamente la memoria, quizás.

Machi-nation

Future part, in archeological museum or warehouse filled with junk, there's a-biomachine-animist. Massive bloated automobile, to complete assigned routine, must continue extracting their blood, as if the donors were a pool of blood, and not specifically anemic beings, beings whose skin sits on their bones, beings licking at marks of usury, with no capacity to run off toward a breaking point, point of no return or potential recycling process. Something that would definitively wipe out memory, maybe.

Local news

Rasante, pasa sobre los edificios que son otras pirámides, donde cada familia reunida es ya lo muerto, sin memoria.

"¡Huye!," como quien dice: "¡huye!" a un ave de corral.

Local news

At a low angle it passes over the buildings that are other pyramids, where each gathered family is that which is already dead, with no memory.

"Run!" like someone saying: "run!" to the poultry.

PeaNut Gallery IV

Entre autistas

"Este paisaje cáustico, la nueva época, la de los tantos crash, los tantos post y las tantas piezas de repuesto".

"Hay una sanguijuela, por la fiebre del oro, en las minas del oro, otras cabezas, otras lenguas se hunden".

"Díriase: el Gran Cañón del ser, cada cual su Gran Cañón del ser, todos los promontorios del ser, desmoronados ya".

"Nada más que agregar".

Among autistics

"This caustic landscape, the new era, the one with so many crashes, all the different 'posts' and a proliferation of spare parts."

"There's a leech, for the gold fever, into the gold mines, other heads, other tongues submerge."

"One might say: the Grand Canyon of essence, to each his own Grand Canyon of essence, all the headlands of one's essence, crumbled."

"Nothing else to add."

Hombre-leopardo

Envejece, sin dejar descendencia y no se acopla al cambio de aquellas piezas por éstas, o al nuevo código del tránsito (una cosa, al mezclarse con la cosa contraria crea lo bastardo y la denominación se ha llenado de bastardos, que deberían pertenecer a otras denominaciones, según sus atributos), envejezco, sin dejar descendencia y no me acoplo al cambio de aquellas piezas por éstas, o al nuevo código del tránsito.

Man-leopard

He ages, leaving no offspring and does not adapt to the exchange of those parts for these parts, or to the new transit rules (one thing, mixing with the opposite thing, produces bastardization, and the naming system has become filled with bastardizations, which should belong to other naming systems, in accordance with their features), I age, leaving no offspring and do not adapt to the exchange of those parts for these parts, or to the new transit rules.

Souvenir

Muñeco negro, en cuya cabeza clavaron alfileres, y aún por entre la ventisca, continúan mis ojos, una linterna a la derecha, una linterna a la izquierda, una linterna a la espalda, rectángulo, un condominio acaso, entro, herramientas al hombro, salgo, y queda atrás la madera.

Souvenir

Black doll, they stuck pins into its head, and even through the blizzard, my eyes keep on moving, a lantern on the right, a lantern on the left, a lantern at my back, rectangle, a condominium perhaps, I go inside, tools across my shoulder, I go back out, and the wood remains behind.

Griot

Hombre-collage.

(Hispano este civil, aunque de origen afro, intenta introducir artefacto en ciudad capital, o en país de inmigrantes, o en país necesitado de mayores y menores vigas.)

Enumeración:

1. casco de micro brigadista
2. cabellera teñida
3. pulóver industrial
4. saya escocesa
5. sandalias manufacturadas
6. bastón
7. rosario
8. barba de patriarca
9. pañoleta
10. otros implementos

Hombre-collage.

(Hispano este civil, aunque de origen afro, intenta introducir artefacto en ciudad capital, o en país de inmigrantes, o en país necesitado de mayores y menores vigas.)

Pero cómo.

Griot

Man-collage.

(Hispanic this civilian, though of Afro origin; attempts to introduce artifact into capital city, or into nation of immigrants, or country in need of large and small load-bearing beams.)

Enumeration:

1. helmet for microbrigade that built this place
2. long dyed hair
3. promotional t-shirt
4. Scots kilt
5. factory-made sandals
6. liturgical staff
7. rosary
8. patriarch's beard
9. schoolchild's kerchief
10. other implements

Man-collage.

(Hispanic this civilian, though of Afro origin; attempts to introduce artifact into capital city, or into nation of immigrants, or country in need of large and small load-bearing beams.)

But how?

Phoenix

Nunca llores por mí si la policía me arresta, quebrantador de la ley, eso fue antes de conocer a Jah.

Estuve en el pudridero de hombres y encontré la avenida, hoy, que podría ser lata de conserva, el horror molido adentro, soy un cosechador tranquilo, en su campo particular y pequeño, existiendo y cantando, dándole muerte al miedo.

Nunca llores por mí si la policía me arresta, quebrantador de la ley, eso fue antes de conocer a Jah.

Estuve en el pudridero de hombres y encontré la avenida, hoy, que podría ser lata de conserva, el horror molido adentro, soy un cosechador tranquilo, en su campo particular y pequeño, existiendo y cantando, dándole muerte al miedo.

Nunca llores por mí si la policía me arresta, quebrantador de la ley, eso fue antes de conocer a Jah.

Dentro y fuera del juego, su atributo exterior, a la vista de todos y su ser interior a la vista de Jah, aquí también está el Rasta.

Phoenix

Don't cry for me if the police arrest me, breaker of the law, that was before I knew Jah.

I was in the man-trash bin and I found the avenue, today, could be a can for the preserves, horror crushed inside, I'm a harvester, calm, on my small specific plot, existing and singing, killing off the fear.

Don't cry for me if the police arrest me, breaker of the law, that was before I knew Jah.

I was in the man-trash bin and I found the avenue, today, could be a can for the preserves, horror crushed inside, I'm a harvester, calm, on my small specific plot, existing and singing, killing off the fear.

Don't cry for me if the police arrest me, breaker of the law, that was before I knew Jah.

Inside and outside the game, its exterior attribute, in sight of all and its interior self in sight of Jah, the Rasta is right here too.

Milord

Caballero, Orden de la Estrella de Down, dama, su realidad con parches,
si hay alguien o algo, entre los extraños seres cómicos, que toda la vida
continúe habiendo alguien o algo, entre los extraños seres cómicos.

Visto que la alegría, es también alimento del hombre, donde véndense
otras raciones de tiempo de guerra, sin embargo.

Caballero, Orden de la Estrella de Down, dama, su realidad con parches,
si hay alguien o algo, entre los extraños seres cómicos, que toda la vida
continúe habiendo alguien o algo, entre los extraños seres cómicos.

Visto que la alegría, es también alimento del hombre, donde véndense
otras raciones de tiempo de guerra, sin embargo.

Caballero, Orden de la Estrella de Down, dama, su realidad con parches,
si hay alguien o algo, entre los extraños seres cómicos, que toda la vida
continúe habiendo alguien o algo, entre los extraños seres cómicos.

En Alamar, en el downtown, yo también dije: "paso, al muy señor
de la risa".

Milord

Knight, Order of the Down Star, lady, his patched reality, if there is
someone or something, among the strange comic beings, may there
always be someone or something in life, among the strange comic beings.

Having seen that happiness, it too is sustenance for man, where other
rations are sold in a time of war, anyhow.

Knight, Order of the Down Star, lady, his patched reality, if there is
someone or something, among the strange comic beings, may there
always be someone or something in life, among the strange comic beings.

Having seen that happiness, it too is sustenance for man, where other
rations are sold in a time of war, anyhow.

Knight, Order of the Down Star, lady, his patched reality, if there is
someone or something, among the strange comic beings, may there
always be someone or something in life, among the strange comic beings.

In Alamar, downtown, I too said: "I give it up, for the very dear lord
of laughter."

El bobo

Máquinas tragamonedas, aunque en las palmas de sus manos no halla
líneas, no se pueda leer el futuro, es una buena persona, debería aquí hablar,
ustedes, deberían oír, máquinas tragamonedas, aunque en las palmas de
sus manos no halla líneas, no se pueda leer el pasado, es una buena perso-,
debería aquí hablar, ustedes, deberían oír, máquinas tragamonedas, aunque
las palmas de sus manos sean mapas blancos, es una buena per-, debería
aquí hablar, ustedes, deberían oír, hombre, con aletas de pez, por si acaso.

The fool

Coin-swallowing machines, though in his palms no lines appear, his future can't be read, he's a good person, he should speak here, all of you, you should hear, coin-swallowing machines, though in his palms no lines appear, his past can't be read, he's a good pers-, he should speak here, all of you, you should hear, coin-swallowing machines, though his palms have no maps, he's a good p-, he should speak here, all of you, you ought to hear, man, with fish flippers, just in case.

El repartidor de biblias

El repartidor de biblias, Dios o su mensajero, va de casa en casa distribuyendo biblias. Ni comida, ni ropa, ni enseres domésticos, ni paquete turístico, ni citación judicial. Hoy, que me llamo Pessoa, mi nostalgia es la botella cuyo contenido era leche, a la puerta dejada. Exiliado de mí, si pudiera regresar a algún sitio, me gustaría regresar a mí mismo, lugar con arboledas. Ni comida, ni ropa, ni enseres domésticos, ni paquete turístico, ni citación judicial. Hoy, que me llamo Pessoa, mi nostalgia es la botella cuyo contenido era leche, a la puerta dejada. Exiliado de mí, si pudiera regresar a algún sitio, me gustaría regresar a mí mismo, lugar con arboledas. Ni comida, ni ropa, ni enseres domésticos, ni paquete turístico, ni citación judicial. Bombas de humo, para que tú en el invisible te conviertas. Algo por los asediados hay que hacer.

The bible distributer

The bible distributer, God or his messenger, goes from house to house handing out bibles. Not food, or clothing, or domestic utensils, or tourist package, or judicial citation. Today, when my name is Pessoa, my nostalgia is for the bottle whose contents were milk, left by the door. Exiled from me, if I could go back to one location, I'd like to go back to my self, location with stands of trees. Not food, or clothing, or domestic utensils, or tourist package, or judicial citation. Today, when my name is Pessoa, my nostalgia is for the bottle whose contents were milk, left by the door. Exiled from me, if I could go back to one location, I'd like to go back to my self, location with stands of trees. Not food, or clothing, or domestic utensils, or tourist package, or judicial citation. Smoke bombs, so you'll turn into the invisible man. Something must be done for the beleaguered.

El extintor

Las campanas repican (el cencerro del pastor amoroso, llamando suave-
mente a las ovejas, para que entren al), por candela, algún día me voy a
convertir en, por candela, algún día me voy a convertir en, por candela,
algún día me voy a convertir en, las campanas repican (el cencerro del
pastor amoroso, llamando suavemente a las ovejas, para que entren al),
por candela, algún día me voy a convertir en, por candela, algún día me
voy a convertir en, por candela, algún día me voy a convertir en, o no: si
sucediera el animal cebado, ¿qué quedaría de mí?

The fire extinguisher

The bells chime (the amorous shepherd's bell, its call to the sheep mellow, so they'll go into), by firelight, some day I'll change into, by firelight, some day I'll change into, by firelight, someday I'll change into, the bells chime (the amorous shepherd's bell, its call to the sheep mellow, so they'll go into), by firelight, some day I'll change into, by firelight, some day I'll change into, by firelight, some day I'll turn into, or not: if the fatted animal were to come, what would become of me?

En el dojo

"Héroe o traidor, según, ha alcanzado la silenciosa serenidad de los muertos, visto que los muertos no molestan, ni evento alguno los puede molestar".

"A cambio de tales operaciones, diríase quirúrgicas, nunca podrá trasmitir a los suyos, cada vez menos suyos, lo que aprendió al desaprender, la nueva piel que ganó al perder la antigua piel".

"Héroe o traidor, según, ha alcanzado la silenciosa serenidad de los muertos, visto que los muertos no molestan, ni evento alguno los puede molestar".

In the dojo

"Hero or traitor, the rumor, he's achieved the silent serenity of the dead,
seeing that the dead don't cause any disturbance, nor can any event
disturb them."

"In return for such operations—he'd say surgical—he'll never be able
to transmit to his people, who are less and less his people, the thing he
learned through unlearning, the new skin he earned by losing the old one."

"Hero or traitor, the rumor, he's achieved the silent serenity of the dead,
seeing that the dead don't cause any disturbance, nor can any event
disturb them."

El leproso

Soy el Emperador del helado, por el sabor domino, mansión horizontal,
con ventanas redondas, de vidrio, casa marina tuve, casa marina tuve,
casa marina, en pueblo de los taladradores tuve, si hubiera un soto, al
menos, soy el Emperador del helado, por el sabor domino, mansión
horizontal, con ventanas redondas, de vidrio, casa marina tuve, casa
marina tuve, casa marina, en pueblo de los taladradores tuve, si hubiera
un soto, al menos, era el Emperador del helado, otro más en el interior
de los muros, paso y suena la campañilla.

The leper

I'm the Emperor of ice cream, I dominate through taste, my mansion
horizontal, its windows nice and round, all shining glass, I owned a
seaside home, owned a seaside home, seaside home, in the superdriller
village owned, if there were a grove, at least, I'm the Emperor of ice
cream, I dominate through taste, my mansion horizontal, its windows
round, all shining glass, I owned a seaside home, owned a seaside home,
seaside home, in the superdriller village owned, if there were a grove, at
least, I was the Emperor of ice cream, one more inside the walls, I go
past and the tiny bell dings.

Los intocables

Los amigos-"colegas", mientras más amigos, enemigos, tengo un amigo barrendero, gran competidor del match, yo, nunca he competido con él, gran competidor del match, él, nunca ha competido conmigo, yo no le envidio las maniobras que él hace, él, no me envidia las maniobras que hago, algo en común nos amista, los amigos-"colegas", mientras más amigos, enemigos, tengo un amigo barrendero.

The untouchables

"Colleague"-friends, the longer they're friends, are enemies, I have a
street-cleaner friend, great competitor in a match, I, I've never competed
with him, great competitor in a match, he, he has never competed with
me, I am not jealous of the maneuvers he makes, he, he isn't jealous
of the maneuvers I make, something we share makes us friends,
"colleague"-friends, the longer they're friends, are enemies, I have a
street-cleaner friend.

El hombre del sombrero de castor

Hay la hormiga roja, con antenas, sin derecho al reposo. Viene y me dice: "no soporto, quisiera irme a otra tierra, a otras gentes, a otros hábitos". Hay la hormiga roja, con antenas, sin derecho al reposo. Vuelve y me dice: "no soporto, quisiera irme a otra tierra, a otras gentes, a otros hábitos". Si soporta la hormiga, que soporte él también, o que trate de irse, o que simplemente se mate, pero que antes de matarse me regale el sombrero de castor.

Man with the beaver hat

The red ant exists, with antennae, without any right to repose. He comes and says to me: "I can't take it, I want to go to a different land, different people, different customs." The red ant exists, with antennae, without any right to repose. He comes back and says to me, "I can't take it, I want to go to a different land, different people, different customs." If the ant can take it, let him take it too, or try to go, or just kill himself, but before he kills himself he should give me the beaver hat.

El guardián de la ermita

El guardián de la ermita se retiró de la ermita, viendo que la ermita se había convertido en vulgar casa de cambio, donde se cambiaban cabezas por cajones de sastre, viendo que los ermitaños se habían convertido en vulgares obreros, hacedores de trajes de boda, total para qué.

The warden of the hermitage

The warden of the hermitage left the hermitage, seeing that the hermitage had turned into an ordinary office for currency exchange, where heads were exchanged for hodgepodge, seeing that the hermits had turned into ordinary workers, makers of wedding dresses, totally pointless.

Sifa

(entonces, escribí aquel poema, por quien verso a verso, como el Cristo, en la cruz, lentamente, se nos iba muriendo. Al menos, eso pensé. Han pasado los años y mi admiración por tal poeta y tal obra se ha trocado en desdén. Otro poema, tal vez no menos justo, hubiese escrito hoy. De todo esto, lo que llaman cultura cubana, el ajiaco y sus viandas, estoy harto y es mejor que me calle, o que me largue de aquí).

Wastepipe

(then I wrote that poem for the one who, line by line, like Christ, on the cross, very slowly, was dying on us. At least that's what I thought. The years have gone by and my admiration for a given poet and a given work has turned to disdain. Today he would have written a different poem, perhaps no less right. This whole business they call Cuban culture, an ajiaco, the stew and all its symbolic foodstuffs, I'm fed up with it, better that I shut up or get out of here.)

Tren a Vegas

Hacia casa de Félix, que sin ser grulla budista, ha logrado la perfecta
humildad, caminar, con pies ligeros, sobre todo, mientras el tren avanza
y queda atrás la ciudad criminosa, parto naranjas y arrojo cáscaras a un
costado de las vías, esto ya es algo.

Train to Vegas

Toward the home of Felix, who without becoming a Buddhist crane, has achieved perfect humility, walking over everything with nimble feet, while the train advances and the crime-ridden city falls behind, I split oranges open and toss peels to one side of the rails, this is already something.

PeaNut Gallery V

El lagarto

Hay un lagarto que a la mañana, hora del recomenzar de lo atroz, tiene
la piel verde y al mediodía cambia su piel de color y a la tarde cambia su
piel de color y hacia el anochecer cambia su piel de color, cíclicamente
también, todavía.

Mago de magia barata, si practico la magia, es porque me gustaría poder
convertirme en un idiota, nada me gusta más que hacer bolitas con mis
fluidos laringonasales y otros fluidos, pegarlas encima de todo lo que
sea soporte, arte matérico, liberación del artista matérico, el único y el
último artista matérico.

Hay un lagarto que a la mañana, hora del recomenzar de lo atroz, tiene
la piel verde y al mediodía cambia su piel de color y a la tarde cambia su
piel de color y hacia el anochecer cambia su piel de color, cíclicamente
también, todavía.

Hay El lagarto.

The chameleon

There's a chameleon that has green skin every morning, when the atrocity starts up again, and at noon it changes color and in the afternoon it changes color and around sunset it changes color, also cyclically, still.

Magician of cheap magic, if I practice magic, it's because I'd like to be able to turn myself into an idiot, nothing gives me more pleasure than rolling little balls with my laryngo-nasal fluids and other fluids, sticking them into everything that could serve as a medium, matter art, liberation of the matter artist, the only and last matter artist.

There's a chameleon that has green skin every morning, when the atrocity starts up again, and at noon it changes color and in the afternoon it changes color and around sunset it changes color, also cyclically, still.

The Chameleon Is.

El estertor

John Keats, bajo árbol se sentaba a leer, cuando le caía en la cabeza,
o en el hombro, el excremento de un pájaro, sonreía, como Buda, como
cualquier niño destructor-constructor de juguetes, yo, bajo árbol me
siento a leer, cuando me cae en la cabeza, o en el hombro, el excremento
de un pájaro, sonrío, como Buda, como cualquier niño destructor-
constructor de juguetes, sangre, otro buche, y debería dejar de fumar,
sangre, otro buche, y debería dejar de escribir.

The death rattle

John Keats, he would sit under a tree to read, when birdshit would
fall on his head, or on his shoulder, he would smile, like Buddha, like
any child destroyer-builder of toys, I, I sit under a tree to read, when
birdshit falls on my head, or on my shoulder, I smile, like Buddha,
like any child destroyer-builder of toys, blood, another bellyful, and
I should quit smoking, blood, another bellyful, and I should quit
writing.

El tibor de hojalata

Artefacto de nieve o muñeco de nieve que construíamos en la breve
nevada habanera, hacia 1992, artefacto de hojalata o tibor de hojalata
que construíamos en la breve nevada habanera, hacia 1992, para coronar
el artefacto de nieve o al muñeco de nieve o a nuestro rey de la nieve,
artefactos de nieve o muñecos de nieve o pretendientes a un trono de
nieve, nosotros también: el artefacto de nieve o el muñeco de nieve
o el rey de la nieve duró lo que duró la nevada habanera, lejano está ya
el año de 1992 y de aquel juego a las consagraciones, sólo queda el tibor
de hojalata.

The tinplate urinal

Snow artifact or snow man we were making in the short Havana
snowfall, around 1992, artifact of corrugated tin or urinal of corrugated
tin we were making in the short Havana snowfall, around 1992, to
coronate the snow artifact or snow man or our king of snows, snow
artifacts or snowmen or pretenders to a snowy throne, us too: the snow
artifact or the snowman or the king of snows lasted as long as the
Havana snowfall lasted, distant now is the year 1992 and of that faraway
game of consecrations the only thing left is the tinplate urinal.

Días de 1834

Leopardi, pasó sus últimos días enceldado, ojillos de ratón tras los
visores observaba el ir y venir de los criados promiscuos, para entonces,
había abandonado todos sus afanes y apenas contestaba al parloteo
de sus interlocutores, sobre la mesa o caja fuerte donde mis propios
órganos percuto otra escenografía que es ruina: moscas panteístas, un
diario, una carta, dirigida al padre mentor, por un adolescente rebelde,
antes de emprender una fuga fallida, sobre la mesa o caja fuerte, donde
mis propios órganos percuto un horóscopo, con unas líneas marcadas a
lápiz, dos vasos vacíos y una botella de ron, por descorchar.

Days of 1834

Leopardi spent his final days in the cell of sickness, little mouse eyes behind visors would observe the coming and going of promiscuous servants, by then he had abandoned all efforts and barely responded to the chattering of interlocutors, on the table or strongbox where my own organs are, I hammer away at another scenario of ruination: pantheistic flies, a diary, a letter, addressed to the mentor by a rebellious adolescent, before launching a failed escape, on the table or strongbox where my own organs are, I hammer away at a horoscope, with a few lines marked in pencil, two empty glasses and a bottle of rum, ready to be opened.

Alemania, 1843

Después de batallar, ese sujeto abyecto, murió tranquilamente, la cara puesta en la madera de la ventana, viendo caer y acumularse la nieve, sobre los mismos sitios donde los dioses transitaron.

Círculos que nunca se completan, nosotros, vamos extinguiendo nuestro tiempo de vida, unas veces hombres exteriores, otras, hombres interiores, sin ser el hombre cabal, de ahí la precariedad de nuestros gestos, círculos que nunca se completan, alguien, en un tiempo más propicio quizás, pueda resolver esta ardua cuestión.

Después de batallar, ese sujeto abyecto, murió tranquilamente, la cara puesta en la madera de la ventana, viendo caer y acumularse la nieve, sobre los mismos sitios donde los dioses transitaron.

Germany, 1843

After battling, that abject individual died peacefully, face resting on the wood of the windowframe, watching the snow fall and pile up, over the same ground traveled by the gods.

Circles never coming to a close, us, we go along wiping out our lifetimes, on some occasions external men, on others internal men, never the man fine and exact, thus the precariousness of our gestures, circles never coming to a close, someone, at a more propitious moment, perhaps, may resolve this arduous issue.

After battling, that abject individual died peacefully, face resting on the wood of the windowframe, watching the snow fall and pile up, over the same ground traveled by the gods.

Dólares canadienses

Tener o no tener dinero, esa es la cuestión. Por la misma época de Arthur Rimbaud, hubo, en Canadá, un joven inmigrante francés que dijo llamarse Arthur Rimbaud. Casó con la joven Emily O'Hara, hija de emigrante irlandés, y juntos fundaron una granja en Whitehorse, a orillas del gran río Yukon. Hoy, sus descendientes son prósperos granjeros y ciudadanos comunes y pacíficos.

Ser poeta es una enfermedad y ser francés es otra enfermedad: Rimbaud, al escapar al África, trató de curar de la enfermedad que es ser poeta y de la enfermedad que es ser francés. De la enfermedad que es ser poeta curó y ahí están sus magras cartas a la hermana Isabel, desde el África, de la enfermedad que es ser francés nunca pudo curar y ahí está su retorno a Marsella y su muerte en hospital de Marsella.

Tener o no tener dinero, esa es la cuestión. Por la misma época de Arthur Rimbaud, hubo, en Canadá, un joven inmigrante francés que dijo llamarse Arthur Rimbaud. Casó con la joven Emily O'Hara, hija de emigrante irlandés, y juntos fundaron una granja en Whitehorse, a orillas del gran río Yukon. Hoy, sus descendientes son prósperos granjeros y ciudadanos comunes y pacíficos.

Canadian dollars

To have or not to have money, that is the question. During the lifetime of Arthur Rimbaud, there was, in Canada, a young French immigrant who said his name was Arthur Rimbaud. He married the young Emily O'Hara, daughter of an Irish emigrant, and together they established a farm in Whitehorse, on the banks of the great Yukon River. Today, their descendents are prosperous farmers and everyday peaceful citizens.

Being a poet is an illness and being French is another illness: Rimbaud, escaping to Africa, tried to recover from the illness of being a poet and from the illness of being French. From the illness of being a poet he recovered, and thus his lean letters to his sister Isabel, from Africa, from the illness of being French he never recovered and thus his return to Marseilles and death in the Marseilles hospital.

To have or not to have money, that is the question. During the lifetime of Arthur Rimbaud, there was, in Canada, a young French immigrant who said his name was Arthur Rimbaud. He married the young Emily O'Hara, daughter of an Irish emigrant, and together they established a farm in Whitehorse, on the banks of the great Yukon River. Today, their descendents are prosperous farmers and everyday peaceful citizens.

La canción del elefante

Soy un elefante, con la trompa endulzada, maestro Pound no traiciona
a país alguno, ladrillos de catedrales o ladrillos de burdeles, los países,
su sitio es el poema, su tiempo es el tiempo del poema, su muerte será
la muerte del poema, soy un elefante, con la trompa endulzada, gracias
doy a ustedes, franciscanos, por confituras caseras, a través de barrotes,
soy un elefante, con la trompa endulzada, maestro Pound no traiciona a
país alguno, ladrillos de catedrales o ladrillos de burdeles, los países, su
sitio es el poema, su tiempo es el tiempo del poema, su muerte sería la
muerte del poema, soy un elefante, con la trompa salada.

The elephant's song

I am an elephant, with my sweet and lucky trunk, master Pound betrays
no country, bricks from cathedrals or bricks from brothels, the countries,
their place is the poem, their time is the time of the poem, their death
will be the death of the poem, I am an elephant, with my sweet and
lucky trunk, I give my thanks to you, Franciscans, for confections made
by hand, passed through iron bars, I am an elephant, with my sweet and
lucky trunk, master Pound betrays no country, bricks from cathedrals or
bricks from brothels, the countries, their place is the poem, their time is
the time of the poem, their death will be the death of the poem, I am an
elephant, my salty trunk all screwed.

El castero

A Fernando Pessoa, le gustaba fumar el tabaco negro de Las Antillas, y el tabaco negro de Las Antillas deja manchas expresionistas en los dientes (la vida y la muerte del portugués genial son la vida y la muerte solitarias de un monje, o un aristócrata, sin rentas, con alguna que otra piedrecilla común, dentro del zapato elitista). A Fernando Pessoa, le gustaba fumar el tabaco negro de Las Antillas, y el tabaco negro de Las Antillas deja manchas expresionistas en los dientes (los poemas del portugués genial son los poemas solitarios de un monje, o un aristócrata, sin rentas, con alguna que otra piedrecilla común, dentro del zapato elitista), porque sí, porque no, porque entre el sí y el no están todos los hombres, a Fernando Pessoa, le gustaba fumar el tabaco negro de Las Antillas, y el tabaco negro de Las Antillas deja manchas expresionistas en los dientes.

A very fine fish

Fernando Pessoa enjoyed smoking black tobacco from the Antilles, and black tobacco from the Antilles leaves expressionist stains on your teeth (the life and death of the brilliant Portuguese are the life and death of a monk, or an aristocrat, without revenues, with one or two common pebbles in an elitist shoe). Fernando Pessoa enjoyed smoking black tobacco from the Antilles, and black tobacco from the Antilles leaves expressionist stains on your teeth (the poems of the brilliant Portuguese are the solitary poems of a monk, or an aristocrat, without revenues, with one or two common pebbles in an elitist shoe), because yes, because no, because between the yes and the no are all men located, Fernando Pessoa enjoyed smoking black tobacco from the Antilles, and black tobacco from the Antilles leaves expressionist stains on your teeth.

Por unas botas tejanas

"Cambiábamos de país como cambiábamos de zapatos", Brecht, antes de ser escritor de la izquierda, comprometido, para decirlo de algún modo, era un hombre cuyo sentido del tacto captaba la aspereza del suelo, si has caminado toda una mañana, sobre asfalto caliente, al mediodía, en tienda por departamentos, te puedes convertir en un místico, viendo unas botas tejanas. "Cambiábamos de país como cambiábamos de zapatos", Brecht, antes de ser escritor de la izquierda, comprometido, para decirlo de algún modo, era un hombre cuyo sentido del tacto captaba la aspereza del suelo, yo, ya que no puedo cambiar de país, quisiera por lo menos poder cambiar de zapatos. ¡Virgen María, que me caiga una plata pa' comprarme unos tacos!

For a pair of Texas boots

"We used to trade out countries like pairs of shoes," Brecht, before he was
a leftist writer, committed to the cause, to say it somehow, he was a man
whose sense of touch registered the unevenness of the ground, if you've
walked for an entire morning, over blazing asphalt, by noon you can
turn mystic in a department store, looking at a pair of Texas boots. "We
used to trade out countries like pairs of shoes," Brecht, before he was a
leftist writer, committed to the cause, to say it somehow, he was a man
whose sense of touch registered the unevenness of the ground, I, since I
can't trade my country, would at least like to trade my shoes. Dear Virgin,
make coin fall from the sky, to buy me some cowboy heels!

Terapia floral

Tomás, sacerdote-poeta, enamorado hasta el húmero de muchacha sufí, antes de la partida, sin mochila esta vez, hacia aldea erigida, bajo claro de luna, donde, atravesando las lianas, filtra luz acuosa que los cuerpos, los motores enfría.

Heterónimo acaso, solitario y tranquilo, cabeza roturada, entre Alamar y Cojímar, sobre puente de hierro, arrojando migajas a los peces comunes, mientras saltan sardinas, recordando a Tomás.

Pedro Marqués, mi amigo, hay cierta tristeza en todo esto, como cuando uno piensa en Buda, después de haber introducido en estómago alcohol.

Floral therapy

Thomas, priest-poet, enamored up to his humerus of a Sufi girl, before his departure, this time without a pack, toward foundational village of the mind, in moonlit clearing where passing through lianas, watery light filters, bringing a chill to bodies, and to motors.

Heteronymous perhaps, solitary and calm, mind churning, between Alamar and Cojímar, over iron bridge, tossing crumbs to the usual fish, as sardines leap, remembering Thomas.

Pedro Marqués, my friend, there's a certain sadness about this whole thing: like when one contemplates Buddha after introducing alcohol to the stomach.

Borges paupau

Pienso en Manuel García, uno de mis antepasados por línea materna, bandolero, a quien llamaron "El Rey de los Campos de Cuba", mientras tomo cerveza y escucho canciones canallescas o creo tomar cerveza y escuchar canciones canallescas pienso en Manuel García, uno de mis antepasados por línea materna, bandolero, a quien llamaron "El Rey de los Campos de Cuba", qué dirán los genetistas, él, tomaba cuanto quería y días hay en que no tengo ni para comprarme una cerveza.

Borges spankspank

Thinking of Manuel García, one of my ancestors on the maternal side, bandit, whom they called "King of the Cuban Countryside," while I drink a beer listening to low-class songs or imagine I'm drinking a beer listening to low-class songs I'm thinking of Manuel García, one of my ancestors on the maternal side, bandit, whom they called "King of the Cuban Countryside," what would geneticists say, he, he drank as much as he wanted and whole days go by when I can't afford one single beer.

La tempestad

Parque, eso es un parque, busto, eso es un busto, 8, ese el número
del muerto, rosquillas a los muertos porque no pueden pistola alguna
disparar, les dicen trovadores provenzales y están cantando canciones de
John Lennon, hubo una época que / hubo una época que / hubo una
época que, parque, eso es un parque, busto, eso es un busto, 8, ese el
número del muerto, rosquillas a los muertos porque no pueden pistola
alguna disparar, les dicen trovadores provenzales y están cantando
canciones de John Lennon, como si fuesen emisiones fónicas del enemigo,
antes estuvieron prohibidas, ahora las pasan por la radio, entre una y otra
balada o mantequilla casera, parque, eso es un parque, busto, eso es un
busto, 8, ese el número del muerto, rosquillas a los muertos porque no
pueden pistola alguna disparar, les dicen trovadores provenzales y están
cantando canciones de John Lennon, hubo una época que / hubo una
época que / hubo una época que, donde todo es a medias y provisional.

The tempest

Park, that's a park, bust, that's a bust, 8, that's the dead man's number,
sweets for the dead because they can't fire off any pistol at all, they're
called Provençal troubadours and they sing John Lennon songs, there
was a time when / there was a time when / there was a time when, park,
that's a park, bust, that's a bust, 8, that's the dead man's number, sweets
for the dead because they can't fire off any pistol at all, they're called
Provençal troubadours and they sing John Lennon songs, as if they were
phonic emissions from the enemy they were prohibited before, now
they're beamed out over the radio, between one ballad and the next or
some bit of strawberry smoothness, park, that's a park, bust, that's a bust,
8, that's the dead man's number, sweets for the dead because they can't
fire off any pistol at all, they're called Provençal troubadours and they
sing John Lennon songs, there was a time when / there was a time when /
there was a time when, where everything's half-assed and temporary.

Los germanistas de "La Casa de Ánimas"

Los germanistas de "La Casa de Ánimas" son unas criaturas simpáticas. Nos hablan de la literatura y las artes alemanas como hablan los forasteros de un lugar del cual, sin embargo, están enamorados. Pienso en los campesinos que tienen barro en las botas.

The Germanists at "The House on All Souls Street"

The Germanists at "The House on All Souls Street" are some friendly creatures. They talk to us about German arts and literature like foreigners talk about a place with which they're somehow enamored. I think about peasants with mud on their boots.

El pensionado

En Alamar, ciudad o pueblecillo semi-campestre, donde no hay cementerio aún, oscuro el hombre cuyo libro de rezos es el manual de botánica, desde que el sol sale, hasta que el sol se pone, entretenido en jardín, quien vio un edificio ya vio todos, es preferible cultivar plantas ornamentales a construir edificios . . .

En Alamar, ciudad o pueblecillo semi-campestre, donde no hay cementerio aún, oscuro el hombre cuyo libro de rezos es el manual de botánica, desde que el sol sale, hasta que el sol se pone, entretenido en jardín, quien vio a una persona ya vio a todas, es preferible cultivar plantas ornamentales a procrear personas . . .

En Alamar, ciudad o pueblecillo semi-campestre, donde no hay cementerio aún, oscuro el hombre cuyo libro de rezos es el manual de botánica, desde que el sol sale, hasta que el sol se pone, entretenido en jardín . . .

The pensioner

In Alamar, city or semi-rural small town, where there's still no cemetery, obscure is the man whose book of prayer is the botanical guide, from the rising of the sun, until the setting of the sun, occupied in garden, whoever has seen one building has seen them all, better to cultivate ornamental plants than raise buildings . . .

In Alamar, city or semi-rural small town, where there's still no cemetery, obscure is the man whose book of prayer is the botanical guide, from the rising of the sun, until the setting of the sun, occupied in garden, whoever has seen one person has seen them all, better to cultivate ornamental plants than breed people . . .

In Alamar, city or semi-rural small town, where there's still no cemetery, obscure is the man whose book of prayer is the botanical guide, from the rising of the sun, until the setting of the sun, occupied in garden . . .

El hombre sobre el sofá

Simplificado, el hombre sobre el sofá, roto ya el hábito de tener una patria, a la gran patria, cuando acabó la guerra, no todos los que partieron quisieron regresar, simplificado, el hombre sobre el sofá, a la gran patria, cuando acabó la guerra, no todos los que partieron quisieron regresar, simplificado, el hombre sobre el sofá

Man on sofa

Simplified, man on sofa, broken now the habit of having a homeland, to the great homeland, after the war ended, not all those who went off wanted to return, simplified, man on sofa, to the great homeland, after the war ended, not all those who went off wanted to return, simplified, man on sofa

EN LA FRONTERA / ON THE BORDERLINE

El contragolpe

Los avestruces ponen los ojos debajo de las alas para no ver el peligro que viene. Los techos se caen y cualquier cosa, de un tiempo a esta parte, es un techo. Arriba abajo a la derecha a la izquierda al frente atrás. Horizontal, sobre arena, el hablante, sangre en la boca, diente aristócrata en escupidera, compatriota. Los avestruces ponen los ojos debajo de las alas para no ver el peligro que viene. Los techos se caen y cualquier cosa, de un tiempo a esta parte, es un techo. Arriba abajo a la derecha a la izquierda al frente atrás. Horizontal, sobre arena, el hablante, sangre en la boca, diente aristócrata en escupidera, compatriota. Los avestruces ponen los ojos debajo de las alas para no ver el peligro que viene. Los techos se caen y cualquier cosa, de un tiempo a esta parte, es un techo. Monólogo, antes del golpe final que lo enviara de cuadrilátero a morgue: "Sólo le pido a Dios, si es que Dios está y no es otra cosa entre tales escombros, que me mantenga con los ojos abiertos, Dios, que me mantengas con los ojos abiertos." Arriba abajo a la derecha a la izquierda al frente atrás. Hip hop hip hop hip hop hip hop hip hop hip hop. Arriba abajo a la derecha a la izquierda al frente atrás. Hip hop hip hop hip hop hip hop hip hop hip hop. Arriba abajo a la derecha a la izquierda al frente atrás. Hip hop hip hop hip hop hip hop hip hop hip hop.

"One, two, three, four, five, six, seven, eight, nine, ¡K.O!"

The counterpunch

Ostriches tuck their eyes under their wings so as not to see the approaching danger. The ceilings are falling in and any thing, from a time to this place, is a ceiling. Up down to the right to the left forward back. Horizontal, on the sand, the speaker, blood in his mouth, aristocratic tooth in spittoon, compatriot. Ostriches tuck their eyes under their wings so as not to see the approaching danger. The ceilings are falling in and any thing, from a time to this place, is a ceiling. Up down to the right to the left forward back. Horizontal, on the sand, the speaker, blood in his mouth, aristocratic tooth in spittoon, compatriot. Ostriches tuck their eyes under their wings so as not to see the approaching danger. The ceilings fall in and anything, from a time to this place, is a ceiling. Monologue, before the final blow that would send him from the ring to the morgue: "I only ask of God, if God is there and it's not something else in the debris, to keep my eyes open, God, keep my eyes open." Up down to the right to the left forward back. Hip hop hip hop hip hop hip hop hip hop hip hop. Up down to the right to the left forward back. Hip hop hip hop hip hop hip hop hip hop hip hop. Up down to the right to the left forward back. Hip hop hip hop hip hop hip hop hip hop hip hop.

"One, two, three, four, five, six, seven, eight, nine, K.O!"

In 1989, Martin Majoor designed a groundbreaking serif typeface, FF Scala, for the Vredenburg Music Center in Utrecht. In 1991, FontFont released the face as FF Scala. It appears in this book, along with its sans serif version for titles.